More About
My Magnificent Machine

More About My Magnificent Machine

William L. Coleman

Bethany Fellowship INC.
MINNEAPOLIS, MINNESOTA 55438

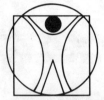

More About My Magnificent Machine

Scripture verses marked TLB are taken from The Living Bible, copyright 1971 by Tyndale House Publishers, Wheaton, Ill. Used by permission.

Published by Bethany Fellowship, Inc.
6820 Auto Club Road, Minneapolis, Minnesota 55438

Printed in the United States of America

Library of Congress Cataloging in Publication Data

Coleman, William L
   More about my magnificent machine.

   SUMMARY: More explanations of basic human physiology with related study questions, Bible quotations, and religious thoughts.
   1. Human physiology—Juvenile literature.   2. Body, Human—Juvenile literature.   3. Children—Religious life—Juvenile literature.
[1. Body, Human.   2. Christian life]   I. Title.
QP37.C6928   612   79-21140
ISBN 0-87123-386-X

**Devotionals for families with young children
by William L. Coleman**

Counting Stars, meditations on God's creation.

My Magnificent Machine, devotionals centered around the marvels of the human body.

Listen to the Animals, lessons from the animal world.

On Your Mark, challenges from the lives of well-known athletes.

The Good Night Book, bedtime inspirationals (especially for those who may be afraid of the dark).

More About My Magnificent Machine, more devotionals describing parts of the human body and how they reflect the genius of the Creator.

Acknowledgment

A special thanks to June Coleman for reading and correcting this manuscript.

Biographical Sketch

WILLIAM L. COLEMAN is a graduate of the Washington Bible College in Washington, D.C., and Grace Theological Seminary in Winona Lake, Indiana.

He has pastored three churches: a Baptist church in Michigan, a Mennonite church in Kansas and an Evangelical Free Church in Aurora, Nebraska. He is a Staley Foundation lecturer.

The author of 75 magazine articles, his by-line has appeared in *Christianity Today, Eternity, Good News Broadcaster, Campus Life, Moody Monthly, Evangelical Beacon,* and *The Christian Reader.* This is Coleman's sixth children's book.

Contents

A NOTE TO PARENTS

Almost all of the chapters in this devotional book are of interest to children of any age (and adults too!). But if your children are quite young, you may wish to skip the chapter at the end called "Growing Up Quickly," which deals with the subject of puberty.

Your Amazing Body!

Blink your eyes, move your arm, whistle. We have amazing bodies. Each time we move, millions of tiny cells carry out difficult jobs just to keep us going. They do this many times every day without our ever thinking about it.

Did our body come together just by chance? That is hard to believe. A body as well made as ours had to have someone design it. The parts had to fit perfectly and move exactly. The person who designed our amazing body is God himself.

As you read I think you will see what a great job God has done. I hope you will also find out who Jesus Christ really is.

William L. Coleman
Aurora, Nebraska

one

You Are Someone Special!

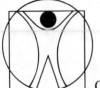 God must have more important things to do than worry about me. Have you ever felt that way? He must be terribly busy. There are so many people, animals, insects and stars to keep track of. How could He care about a young person living in your neighborhood?

No doubt, God is very busy. If all He had to do each day was to take care of the stars alone, He would have a full-time job.

Some clear evening count the stars. If you are seeing at your best, you might be able to count 2,000 or more. That would be plenty to take care of. But scientists tell us there are millions and billions more. There are at least 200 billion, billion stars.

How long would it take you to count that high? Without a computer it would take a very long time. Probably you'd become tired and never get it done.

The Bible tells us that God not only counts the stars but that He also calls each of them by name. He knows what is going on with each of those billions of stars.

Stars are no little things to care about. For instance, the sun is a star, but it isn't a little ball of fire in the air. The sun is so large the earth would fit into the sun over one million times.

That sounds big. Yet, it is only a start. The sun is only a medium-sized star. Many stars are much larger. One star is over 1,000 times bigger than the sun. Can you even imagine how big that is?

If we think about all these sizes and numbers, the earth doesn't seem very large. So how can God care about it? On the earth there are billions of people. With this much to watch over, can God possibly care about you?

God not only cares but He thinks that you are someone special. He knows what you had for breakfast today. He knows what your favorite color is and what kind of games you like to play.

You and I couldn't do that because there would be too much to remember. God's mind is not like ours. He can remember, think, and care about billions of things all at one time.

Today when you smile God will know about it. He might even smile with you. When you are working hard He might help you to get it done. When you eat your lunch He will be sitting next to you.

God knows the name of a star that is 4 1/2 light years away (Alpha Centurai). He also knows your name—even your middle name.

"When I look up into the night skies and see the work of your fingers—the moon and the stars you have made—I cannot understand how you can bother with mere puny man, to pay any attention to him" (Ps. 8:3, 4, TLB).

1. How many stars are there?
2. How big is the sun?
3. Name three people who care about you.

God knows and cares.

two
Heartbeat

 Have you ever checked out your heartbeat? You can feel it pounding if you touch just the right spot.

The place most of us use to check our heartbeat is our wrist. If we place our fingers lightly on the thumb side of our inside left wrist, we can feel the heartbeat. Even though we feel our heartbeat there, that is not the place where it begins. The beat we feel in our wrist actually began in our heart and as quick as a wink moved into our arm.

Heart or pulse beats move through the body like vibrations. If you flick one end of a rubber band, the movement travels across it. This is a vibration. The heart beats and the wrists move.

The wrist is the most popular place to feel a heartbeat, but it is not the only part of the body that pulsates. The side of our neck also has a strong beat. So does the side of our head, and the area above our ankles.

A baby's heart beats twice as fast as that of an adult. Every minute it pounds 130 to 150 times. At 6 years of age it slows down to around 100 beats a minute. At 10 years of age it slows to about 90. Adult men should be beating at 70 times a minute. The heartbeat of a woman is a little higher, about 78 times per minute.

The number of beats will change, depending upon our health and what we are doing. When a person lies down the pulse slows. If he plays ball it starts to race. An excellent athlete in good health, with strong muscles, may have a slower heartbeat.

When the first astronauts were in the rocket ship and about to be launched into space, their heartbeats were not fast. Their pulses were beating more slowly than some of the people watching them on television. They were healthy, they knew what they were doing and were able to relax.

The pulsebeat in animals differs greatly from man. A huge elephant may have a heart rate of only 25 to 50 times per minute. Your cat's pulse is somewhere between 120 and 140. The tiny hummingbird has a beat ten times faster than men. It races at 800 to 1,000 times a minute or 13 times each second.

One way to check the speed of a heartbeat is to put your fingers on the wrist and count the beats for half a minute. Then double the number and you will have it. Most of us, however, do not check our own heartbeat very well.

The heart is our main machine. If it stops beating, all our other parts will also soon quit working. The heart pumps the blood which keeps everything else working.

A man once asked Jesus Christ what was the most important thing man could do. He said we have to love God from our main machine, our heart.

"Love the Lord your God with all your heart, soul, and mind" (Matt. 22:37, TLB).

He was saying: don't love God a little bit. Not even halfway. Love God with everything you have.

1. How many times does the hummingbird's heart beat every minute?
2. When you were a baby, how many times did your heart beat every minute?
3. Why did Jesus use the word heart?

The more we know about God the more we love Him.

three

Why Two Ears Are Better

 When we become teenagers many of us begin to notice our ears more. For a while we think they are too large. Most of the time we think they are the right size, but after a while we forget about them.

We ignore our ears most of our lives except for a regular cleaning and an occasional earache. However, many people do have serious problems with their hearing. A few cannot hear at all, but many more are limited. There may be six million people in the United States who have hearing problems.

Young people usually hear well. They can hear sounds which are very low and extremely high. Often the younger the person is, the better he can pick up sound.

When we grow older our ability to hear changes. After age 60 most people are not able to hear as well. The high sounds which come from some record players are lost to those who are older. The tissue in the ear probably does not move as well as it used to.

An ear is naturally a big help, but why do we need two of them? We have only one nose and one tongue. If we had only one ear we could still get along well. Probably we could hear almost as much with one ear as with two.

The real reason we need two ears is for the purpose of discerning direction. If a car drives behind your back, you can follow its movement. You hear it coming, you can tell when it is directly behind you, and you can hear it leaving. With only one ear you could hear it get loud and soft but would have trouble understanding from which direction it was going or coming.

It would be hard to know if something was on your right side or your left without two good ears. If an ambulance were coming, it would take you longer to know which way to move.

If you lost your ability to hear extremely high sounds, you wouldn't have lost much. Some sounds are just a bother anyway. But if you lost the complete hearing in one ear, you would have a more serious problem. It really pays to take care of your health and keep your hearing sharp.

Worse than the person who is unable to hear is the person who can hear but doesn't want to. Imagine someone hearing a train whistle but deciding to walk on the track anyway. Suppose a person hearing a fire alarm still refused to leave the burning building.

The Bible is filled with good advice for young people. Some parts, like the book of Proverbs, are written specifically for youth. King Solomon tells young people how to avoid a great deal of disappointment and heartache. He also shows them how to stay away from sin which will hurt themselves and others. But, too often we hear the words but pay no attention to them.

"A wise man will hear, and will increase learning; and a man of understanding shall attain unto wise counsels" (Prov. 1:5, KJV).

1. Why do we need two ears?
2. How many people in the U.S. have a hearing problem?
3. Which book in the Bible is especially good for young people?

We need to hear well the good advice of God.

four

The Tricky Appendix

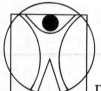 Do you still have your appendix? One person out of ten has trouble with his appendix at one time or another. Often the trouble becomes so serious that the appendix has to be removed.

Where is your appendix and what value does it have? For most of us the appendix is located about halfway between our navel and our right hip bone. But that is only for most of us. It can be located much higher, much lower, or even on the left side of our bodies.

The appendix isn't a large part of your body. It is about the length of your little finger. It could be a little thinner, but that gives you some idea of its relative size. This small worm-like section hangs from the intestine like a loose string on a sweater sleeve.

In some ways the appendix is a simple organ and easy to understand, but in other ways doctors feel that it holds many mysteries. Some scientists feel that the appendix used to serve a good purpose but that it is no longer important to the body. Others feel that the appendix does the same job it has always done. It works in the same way as our tonsils. If a harmful food or chemical gets into our body, the appendix works like a smoke alarm. It warns the rest of our body. "Get ready—here comes trouble" is the message. This allows the rest of the body to send out special fighters to beat back the harmful chemicals.

Once in a while the appendix becomes flooded. There are more germs than it can handle. When this happens the appendix enlarges and gets sick. This enlargement is called appendicitis.

When the appendix becomes enlarged you might feel the pain in another section of your body. The only person who can really decide whether or not you have a sick appendix is a doctor, so be sure you see a doctor if you have trouble in this area. If an appendix is allowed to swell too much, it could burst.

Most of the time the appendix will continue doing its job. If it has to be removed, other parts of the body will automatically take over.

The amazing thing is that there are safeguards and alarm systems in your body. God gave them to you for your protection. You don't have to tell them when to work—they just take over.

Fortunately, the protective parts of your body do not sleep or take vacations. They are always on guard and busy. The same thing can be said of God. He watches over your life without sleeping or going on vacation.

God wants to warn you when you get too close to doing some evil. He wants to pull you back when you start to plan something that may hurt you. There are some things we don't see as being bad, so He tries to warn you before it is too late.

"Jehovah himself is caring for you! He is your defender. He protects you day and night" (Ps. 121:5, 6, TLB).

1. Where is your appendix?
2. What is its job (probably)?
3. How does God warn us?

Thanks for watching over us.

five

Swallowing Upside Down

Have you ever thought that your throat was similar to a metal pipe? You merely place the food in your mouth, push it back to this pipe and feel the food drop into your stomach. This idea is far from the truth. Your throat is a very interesting and intricate structure.

Lining the throat are strong muscles which help to do amazing things. If you stood on your head, you could still eat a sandwich. Perhaps it wouldn't be the most comfortable lunch you had ever eaten, but it could be done.

Before a person sends food back to the throat, he needs to chew it into tiny pieces. Food can be swallowed better and digested in the stomach more easily if it has been chewed well.

After the food is chewed, the tongue pushes it against the roof of the mouth moving it toward the throat. As this is being done the holes leading to the nose close, preventing food from entering that section.

Fortunately, God has made the human body in a wonderful way so that the right places close on time. Air travels up and down part of the same hallway in which food travels. That is why a special trapdoor called the epiglottis (epi-glot-tis) closes just as those strong muscles push food through the throat. This door stops food from going into the windpipe and lungs.

If a piece of food gets past this door accidentally a person will know it right away. He will start to choke and cough as he tries to throw it back out. This can be painful.

Not everyone knows all the parts of the throat, but many of us know what it is like to choke. It is a miserable feeling and usually makes us red in the face.

Not only do people and animals choke, but plants do also. Weeds often grow too close to plants, choking out their life until they die.

Jesus told a story about choking. He said some of us worry too much about ourselves. We are busy trying to get things and have no time to help others. He said we are being choked by selfishness. We are acting like hogs, just eating up everything for ourselves.

He wants us to start looking out for others. Selfishness chokes.

"Whose faith is choked out by worry and riches and the responsibilities and pleasures of life. And so they are never able to help anyone else to believe the Good News" (Luke 8:14, TLB).

1. What is one cause of choking?
2. What is the little door called?
3. How did Jesus say we might choke?

Selfishness is our big enemy.

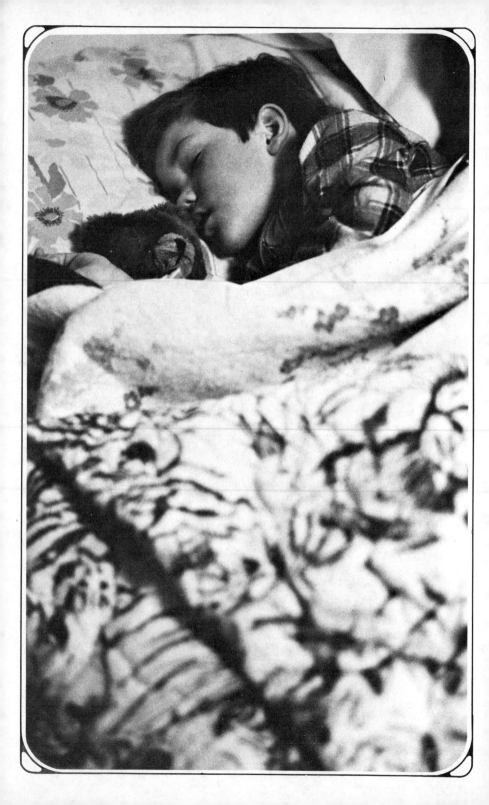

six

How Much Sleep?

 Most children hate to go to bed. They try to talk their parents into letting them stay up later. It seems silly to have to sleep so much. During our lifetimes, we will sleep a total of 24 years—one-third of our life.

Scientists have discovered some interesting facts about sleep. There seem to be four parts to sleep: light sleep, deep sleep, deeper sleep, and deepest sleep. These four stages may be repeated several times in one night. A person does not sleep at one level all night long.

Once in a while someone will get up and walk around while he is sleeping. Sleepwalking is dangerous because the person might fall down the steps or crash into a window. Someone should wake up the sleepwalker and get him back into bed. Scientists believe sleepwalking is usually caused by worry or fear.

The amount of sleep you need depends upon who you are. For some people, eight hours is just right. Others need ten or possibly just six. As we grow into adults we learn to figure out how much we need. Children are better off letting their parents figure it out. During the important growing years, plenty of sleep is a big help.

While we are sleeping our body stands guard like a watchdog. Our eyes and ears are still sending messages. Ears still hear all the noise in the room or the cars driving past the house. Our eyes are saying, "It is dark in here with no lights and my lids closed." Your body can feel the comfort of the bed and the warmth of the covers.

There is a big difference in our brain, however. During sleep it shuts down some of its departments. Most of the messages coming from our fingers, eyes and ears are simply ignored. The brain is busy handling our dreams and maybe storing our memories.

If there is a sudden change, though, our brain is immediately alert and ready for work. If the telephone rings, our brain takes the message and notifies our body.

Perhaps you have walked from one bed to another during the night without waking up. Then your parents led you by the hand and tucked you back into your own bed. The next day you didn't remember anything about that trip. It was your brain that started you on that trip even though your parents had to end it for you.

A good night's sleep is a beautiful gift from God. After we are well rested, the next day will be a whole lot happier and smoother. So let's ask God to take care of our problems tonight while we get a good night's rest.

"If you sit down, you will not be afraid; when you lie down, your sleep will be sweet" (Prov. 3:24, KJV).

1. Can we hear when we're asleep?
2. How long do you sleep in a lifetime?
3. How do you feel if you haven't slept enough?

Sleep is one of God's biggest helps.

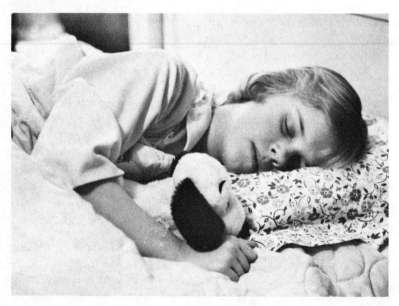

seven

Walking in Circles

 Do you walk straight? Think before you answer that one. Most of us want to say yes right away. After all, we don't walk into walls or bump into each other much. But no matter how it seems to us, almost no one walks in a straight line.

Try an experiment. Tie a blindfold on a member of your family and ask him to walk a straight line. After just a few steps, he will start to go toward the left or the right. Ask a friend and see how surprised he is.

The reason for walking in circles is rather easy. We are not as straight and well balanced as we might think.

Look at people's shoulders and notice how many are leaning to one side or another. Watch people walk. Their steps are usually not even. We may place more weight on one foot or take a slightly longer step with the other.

Some find it difficult to walk very far simply because their steps are so different. We call the way we walk our gait. The gait of one person may be entirely different from his neighbor's.

The other thing which causes us to wander in a circle is our weight. Often one side of our body weighs more than the other side. Our heart is on our left side and our small appendix is on our right. Our legs may vary in size also, as well as our arms.

Without seeing where we are going, most of us will slowly move to the left or right, eventually walking in a complete circle.

A line may be drawn in front of us, but if we close our eyes we will soon get off it. We start to wander. The same thing happens when we follow Jesus Christ. If we take our eyes off Him and what He has taught us, we will soon be wandering around, confused. We need to keep our eyes on our goal if we don't want to stumble around.

25

"I have tried my best to find you—don't let me wander off from your instructions" (Ps. 119:10, TLB).

1. Why don't we walk in a straight line?
2. What is our gait?
3. What happens if we wander away from Christ?

Keep my entire life from going in circles.

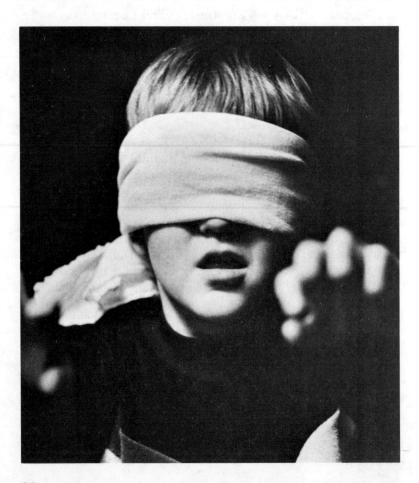

eight
The Healthy Sun

 Being in the sun is fun. Even on cold days we seem to feel warmer just because the sun is shining. Actually it is more than just a feeling. The sun's purpose is to make us healthier and happier.

For instance, everyone needs vitamin D. Although some food products supply vitamin D, sunshine is the best way of getting it. Just by shining on our body the sun causes vitamin D to increase in us. There is no need to eat something or even swallow a pill. The vitamin D just soaks into our skin. The sun supplies it through ultraviolet rays. This is why we call vitamin D the "sunshine vitamin."

The sun does more for us. Sunshine helps kill bacteria and fungi which live on our skin. Because the sun helps destroy germs on the skin, the body has added strength to fight disease inside the body. Even though you may get sunshine only on your face and arms, this is still a big help.

Scientists are still studying the many ways in which the sun helps our health. They can see what the sun does even if they do not entirely understand how it is done.

The body has a special set of white blood cells. These cells defeat disease. Somehow sunshine causes these cells to become more active and do a better job.

Some people even believe that sunshine helps our muscles. It seems to tighten the muscles and give them added strength.

Doctors have found that sunlamps seem to improve the health of people who are shut-ins. With a sunlamp they can get ultraviolet rays for short periods of time.

Another good thing about sunshine is that it makes us think better. After a person has been in the dark indoors or gone through a long, cloudy winter, the sun seems to wake him up and make him want to do things.

We have to be careful with ultraviolet rays and too much sunshine, however. Like everything else, too much can be harmful. But in just the correct amounts sunshine makes our body work even better.

We realize that the sun is good. It helps food grow and gives health to our body. Almost 3,000 years ago the Psalmist David was thinking about God and how good He was. Then he said to himself that God is so good He reminds me of the sun.

God is like the sun. He wants to help us. He gives us a happier outlook on life and protects us from evil. We become stronger just knowing He is around.

"For the Lord God is a Sun" (Ps. 84:11, KJV).

1. What rays are given by the sun?
2. What vitamin comes from the sun?
3. How is God like the sun?

Thank God for shining down on us.

nine

A Good Memory

 Most people are smarter than they think and could improve their brain power simply by using it more. If people practice remembering things they may become much better at it.

Many children have trouble memorizing, especially if they have to learn spelling words or memorize a times table. Yet, some of them know the batting averages of every major league baseball player. These averages change every day and still kids can know them.

Sometimes you might get behind in school and feel like giving up. You figure it's no use. Perhaps you even think of yourself as "dumb." This is far from true. You just haven't begun to use that great brain you are carrying around.

Just imagine for a minute that you were an animal or an insect. If you were a jellyfish, you wouldn't have any brain at all. Suppose you had the brain of a tiny flatworm. As small as they are, they still use their sight and handle a little bit of information.

A green lizard may look dumb but it isn't. They have complicated brains and can react to many things. Fish seem to "think" with their noses. A salmon has a good sense of smell. They can even find their part of the ocean merely by sniffing it out.

For some reason God did not make us like animals. We have excellent brains and outstanding memories. Our memories seem to be so good that even after having part of our brain removed in surgery most of us could still remember well.

Memory is much like a tape recording. If I record the information well, I can play it back better the next time. The mind is like a gigantic tape rack. Conversations, pictures, stories, addresses, and numbers are all recorded and stored. Later, when I need them my computer brain selects the correct tape and plays it again for me. The better I record the material and the more often I play it the better my memory will become.

Remembering is like throwing a baseball. The more we practice the better we can do it.

It is difficult to know how many people have lived on the earth. Certainly, many billions! In God's tremendous "brain," He can remember each one of us by name. He remembers the color of our hair and eyes and doesn't forget what kind of dessert we like. He also practices His memory by thinking about us often.

"Then he said, 'Jesus, remember me when you come into your Kingdom.' And Jesus replied, 'Today you will be with me in Paradise. This is a solemn promise' " (Luke 23:42, TLB).

1. Describe the brain of a jellyfish.
2. Why do most of us have poor memories?
3. Can you name anything God "forgets"?

Thanks for remembering us and forgetting our sins.

ten

What Are Germs?

 Have you ever seen a germ? We can't see them without a strong microscope. Germs are tiny plants which are alive. When they get into a body they can cause sickness and disease.

A close relative of the germ is the virus. Viruses can be seen with a special electronic microscope.

Don't feel badly if you have never seen a germ; most people haven't. In fact, a hundred years ago most doctors and scientists didn't even believe that germs existed. Now doctors realize that some people get sick, become crippled, and even die because of little germs.

Germs are traveling all the time, hoping to find a place to rest. When someone sneezes, thousands of germs fly through the air. Many germs could be lying around the house mixed in the dust or carried in by people.

Some germs get inside people by insect bites. Years ago one of the most dangerous insects was the mosquito. Many thousands of people died because of germs carried by the mosquito. Thank God this has changed.

Another carrier of germs is a certain type of flea. In the olden days a flea would first live on a mouse and then later bite a person. The germs it gave to the human killed thousands of people in Europe.

Germs are also found in food. We are fortunate to live in a time when we understand about germs. Our vegetables, milk and eggs are usually germ free.

No matter how careful we are, though, germs still get into our body. We often breathe germs in through the nose and mouth. At

other times we shake hands with someone and then place the same hand on our face.

When a germ gets inside our body it can hurt us in a number of ways. Some germs put poison into our bloodstream while others destroy the tiny tissues in our body.

If germs are coming into our body every day, why aren't we sick all the time? The biggest reason is because healthy bodies can fight off most germs. By eating and sleeping correctly our body is able to fight and destroy these unwelcome enemies. A few germs are too strong for our system to defeat and then we get medicine to wipe them out.

God has given us a body so we can serve Him. When we become Christians, the Holy Spirit comes inside us and makes it His home. We need to be as careful as we possibly can with our body. Sometimes we can't avoid sickness, but by eating, sleeping and exercising correctly we will do our best.

"Haven't you yet learned that your body is the home of the Holy Spirit God gave you; and that he lives within you? Your own body does not belong to you" (1 Cor. 6:19, TLB).

1. Why has God given us a body?
2. Why do parents want us to wash our hands?
3. Where does the Holy Spirit live?

Help my body to fight germs.

eleven
Looking Inside

My son had broken his collarbone for the third time. Each time it was in a different place. He had been running and was pushed. When he landed on his shoulder it caused his collarbone to break.

Soon we were sitting in the doctor's office waiting to see the X-ray pictures. It was easy to see the break. A fine line went through the bone showing the injury. The doctor put the arm in a sling and told us to come back in a few weeks.

The X-ray pictures were a big help. Instead of trying to guess how badly it was broken, we could actually see it.

Before X-ray machines were invented, it was much harder to know what was wrong with a patient. They may have had a serious pain but doctors could only guess as to why. Now doctors can take pictures of almost any part of our body.

Dentists use X-ray machines often. Maybe you have seen the small pictures of your teeth and gums. With these pictures the dentist can see tiny decays he otherwise might miss.

X rays do a particularly good job at checking out bones. Bones show up clearly and any damage done to them can be seen fairly easily.

The stomach, liver and kidneys do not show up as well in X-ray pictures so doctors figured out another way. Now before having a stomach X ray a person must drink a special liquid which sometimes tastes terrible. The pictures will come out clearly, however, because the X-ray machine can see the color of the liquid.

Doctors have been taking chest X rays for a long time. These pictures have helped greatly in fighting cancer, emphysema and tuberculosis.

Many lives have been saved with these pictures. The doctor may find an unusual lump or bump inside our body. He can then recommend treatment before the sickness goes too far.

X rays have also proven helpful in checking heart problems. Pictures often show if the heart is oversized, out of shape, or even in the wrong place.

It would be interesting to see what we look like inside. Would you like to know what your stomach looks like or maybe your brain?

Years before the X-ray machine was invented someone was already looking inside of people. God has always been able to see what we are really like. He not only checks out our organs and bones, He knows our thoughts, fears, hopes and dreams.

Because God knows us so well, He is able to help us. He knows us better than we know ourselves.

"Search me, O God, and know my heart; test my thoughts" (Ps. 139:23, TLB).

1. Why do dentists take X rays?
2. What help are X-ray pictures of organs?
3. How does it help when God knows your fears?

Thanks for knowing my thoughts.

twelve

Why Do You Blush?

 Don't you hate to blush? You are trying to be calm and then all of a sudden your face turns red. Almost as red as cherries.

What causes this? There are tiny blood vessels in our face and neck. Quickly they can change size without our asking them to. This is called an involuntary action—an action which we don't have much control over even if we wanted to.

Imagine that you have just been embarrassed. Maybe your uncle said you were cute or handsome and since there were other people around, your face lit up like a Christmas light.

You didn't need a mirror to know you were blushing. Your face felt warm or even puffy like a balloon.

Those tiny blood vessels started moving the second you heard your uncle. You probably couldn't have stopped them no matter how you tried. The vessels dilated. This means they became larger.

And sometimes the blood vessels take their time going down again. It might take them three to five minutes to go back to their normal size.

Suppose you were not just embarrassed, though. Let's pretend you were really frightened. Maybe even shocked. In this case these same vessels would become smaller. When they do this, there is less blood in your face and you turn white or pale. If these vessels become too small too quickly, the blood can be slowed to your brain, causing you to faint.

A person's face can turn red when he is embarrassed or ashamed. If you took some money which wasn't yours and your parents found out, how would you feel? For most of us those

blood vessels would become huge and our face would quickly light up. It is better to live in a way which will not cause us to be ashamed.

Some day we will all meet Jesus. If we believe in Him and have followed Him well, we won't have to blush when we meet Him. It will be exciting and enjoyable—just like meeting a friend and the Son of God at the same time.

"And now, little children, stay in happy fellowship with the Lord so that when he comes you will be sure that all is well, and will not have to be ashamed and shrink back from meeting him" (1 John 2:28, TLB).

1. What makes us blush?
2. Why do we turn pale?
3. Why will you not be ashamed when you meet Christ?

It sounds like a great meeting.

thirteen

How to Get Twins

 Twins must have fun playing tricks on people. They can pretend to be the other one and sometimes keep a teacher guessing. Sometimes they can fool their friends at parties or even while playing a game.

There are many twins in the world. Most of them are never noticed, however, because they usually don't look alike. One out of every ninety-two births turns out to be twins. But how does it happen and why do some look alike while others do not?

The twins which look alike are called identical twins. It is difficult to tell them apart because they are always two boys or two girls. Identical twins are never a girl and a boy.

These twins begin just like other children, as a tiny egg cell (called an ovum). After the father's sperm reaches the egg, the cell divides in half. (Everyone else's egg stays together.) As a result there are two eggs and there will be two children.

The other type of twins happens more often. They are called fraternal twins. Usually a woman produces one egg cell each month. But sometimes she will have two eggs at the same time. If both of these eggs receive sperm from the father, two children could be born.

Fraternal twins are different. They do not look the same and one can be a girl while the other is a boy. There are more fraternal twins than identical twins.

Once in a great while we will see a wide stroller with three cute babies in it. Triplets do not happen often. Only one in 9,000 births produces three children at the same time.

Four children are sometimes born at once, called quadruplets. This happens only once in every half million births.

Five children at one birth is even more rare. This happens once in every 40 million births. There are only a few families in which five have grown to be adults.

It can be especially difficult to have two or more children born at once. One problem is that they are often born too early. Instead of staying inside the mother for the full nine months, they are born a few weeks sooner. This may mean they weigh less and have a harder time at first.

God's world is filled with happy surprises. Sometimes the weather jumps from dreary to a bright, sparkling sun. At other times you go to sleep and wake up with beautiful snow covering the ground.

Parents look forward to having a bouncing baby and they are happily surprised with twins.

We may never have twins but we can still see how generous God can be. For most of us He gives far more than we really need.

"Then, when Job prayed for his friends, the Lord restored his wealth and happiness! In fact, the Lord gave him twice as much as before" (Job 42:10, TLB).

1. What are twins called that don't look alike?
2. What are twins called that look almost exactly alike?
3. How did God help Job?

Thanks for the happy surprises!

fourteen

As We Live and Breathe

 Aren't you glad you don't have to think before you breathe? Out, in, out, in, out. If we had to think in order to breathe, we wouldn't have time for anything else.

Every day a person has to breathe over 15,000 times. He might miss a few or take a couple of extra ones, but this number is fairly close. It wouldn't be much fun to count them just to find out.

The body enjoys air. Air is necessary for producing energy for the body. When air comes inside, it is made up mostly of nitrogen and oxygen. The body uses some of the oxygen. When the nitrogen is exhaled, some oxygen and carbon dioxide also leave. Each breath uses the gases and then sends them out again.

While you are reading this chapter, you are breathing one pint of air with each breath. If you look at a pint-size box of milk, you can see how much air that is. It is certainly enough to keep us alive. However, our body was made to handle over seven pints every time we breath. If we don't get enough exercise and work, our body doesn't take in all the air it was made to handle.

It may be different for some, but most of us breathe 14 times each minute.

Naturally, we can't live without air. But not all air is the same. Some of it is too cold. Around fires the air can be too hot and hurt a person's lungs. In the mountains, air can be too thin. Often the air is far too dirty.

If you have been high in the mountains, you know about this air. In the Colorado Rockies hikers often have to sit down and rest. They have become dizzy from the thin air.

The higher we get the less oxygen there is in the air. Our body needs oxygen and it doesn't get enough. The more we move, climb, or exercise, the more oxygen we need. One of the first parts to suffer is our brain. It isn't receiving enough oxygen to let it work and think well. Often we become sick to our stomach.

When we change our activities most bodies get used to the "thin" air and we can enjoy the mountains.

We don't usually worry about air. You didn't wake up this morning and say, "I hope there is enough air today." Air is just there and it always will be if we don't ruin it.

Every once in a while we should stop and thank God for giving us air so plentiful. If it ever ran out, life would soon come to an end.

That is the way God is. He gives so many things we don't even stop to think about.

"Let every thing that hath breath praise the Lord. Praise ye the Lord" (Ps. 150:6, KJV).

1. What two things make up air?
2. How many times do we breathe in and out every day?
3. Name two other things we forget to thank God for.

We have never seen air but we see what it does. We have never seen God but we see what He does.

fifteen

Visiting the Doctor

 Our family goes to three excellent doctors. They all work in the same building. If one is absent we always know the other two will be there.

We know our doctors well. We feel relaxed with them. If there is something we don't understand, we aren't afraid to ask them about it. We know they care enough to take time to answer us.

Many people are afraid of doctors. They wear white coats and carry instruments which are strange to us. While examining us, doctors sometimes do things we don't understand.

Doctors are like other people. They can be kind, helpful and patient. Once in a while you meet a grumpy one, but there are grumpy mechanics, sales clerks and teachers also.

A doctor has to attend school for many years. First he has to complete four years of college and get excellent grades. Then he must attend four years of medical school. After that he takes training as an "intern." During internship, doctors practice in hospitals. If they do all of this well and pass their examinations, they will become licensed doctors. It takes at least ten years and many thousands of dollars to complete this training. Besides this, most doctors take a few classes throughout their lives.

Because of this training, doctors know a great deal. They understand what a high temperature means. If you have a pain in your side, they know what to look for. If you have a headache which won't stop, they know what to check for.

We live longer today because of trained doctors and good medicine. As they learn more, your children may live even longer and healthier lives.

Many doctors are family physicians. They take care of men, women and children. They handle most common cases of sickness. Once in a while we need something special done. Maybe it is an ear operation or a special set of X rays. In these cases doctors often send us to other doctors called "specialists." They have gone to school for more than ten years and studied a particular part of medicine.

One group of specialists are called pediatricians. They take care of children and babies.

Because of kind, educated doctors many of us will enjoy good health for years to come.

Sometimes we have troubles which are not physical. We feel badly because someone is picking on us. Maybe your parents have been arguing. Possibly your best friend has stopped talking to you.

It is possible to hurt inside and no one will know about it. Sometimes people go to bed and cry and no one finds out. Jesus Christ doesn't just care about your body. He cares about your secrets and what you feel like inside.

Maybe tonight you can tell Him what is bothering you. Then ask Him to help you do something about it.

"He has sent me to heal the brokenhearted" (Luke 4:18, TLB).

1. How long do doctors go to school?
2. What is a pediatrician?
3. Can you remember a time when you really felt badly? What did you do about it?

God reaches inside our hearts and minds.

sixteen

The Sugar Problem

 "You aren't going to add more sugar to that?" The father held his spoon still. He wasn't used to hearing his son talk this way.

"Read the box," continued his 11-year-old boy. "See how much sugar is already in the cereal."

Children are learning that too much sugar is bad for us and now they are teaching their parents. The price we pay for eating too much sugar is decayed teeth and unhealthy bodies.

Some sugar is good for us. It supplies calories which turn into energy. However, most of us eat twice as much sugar as our bodies need. How much sugar do you think most of us eat every year? Is it 10 pounds, 25 pounds, 50 pounds, or 100? The average person in the United States eats 100 pounds of sugar every year.

Sugar doesn't merely come in spoonfuls at breakfast. All day long we seem to be stuffing sugar into our mouth. Candy bars, donuts, jelly, and soda pop are all packed with sugar. Some people have become so worried about the problem they have tried to give up sugar altogether.

Scientists tell us that sugar often gets in the way of more important foods. We get full from eating sweets and then don't care to eat the things we need for good health.

There is also great concern over what sugar does to our teeth. This is especially true when we eat sugar between meals. When sugar is in our mouth, saliva turns it into acid. If this isn't brushed or washed away, it can start to "eat" into our teeth.

This is why between meal snacks are so dangerous. Most people who eat a candy bar in the afternoon usually don't take time to brush their teeth. The next best thing then is to wash out the mouth with water. (Most of us are not likely to do this either.)

Since children enjoy candy and other sweets, they would be much better off to eat them for dessert after meals. Then they are more likely to brush their teeth well and cut down the danger of tooth decay.

Sometimes people have tooth decay which is not their own fault. Their teeth may be weak. For most people, however, this is not the case. Most teeth have problems because they are not taken care of.

The Bible says we usually pay for our sins. If we don't exercise, our bodies become weak. If we don't get enough sleep, we have trouble thinking correctly. If we don't brush our teeth, they decay and need fillings or have to be pulled.

The person who does something wrong usually must pay for it. Before you do something foolish, do yourself a favor—stop and ask how you might be hurting yourself.

"For everyone shall die for his own sins—the person eating sour grapes is the one whose teeth are set on edge" (Jer. 31:30, TLB).

1. When is the best time to eat candy?
2. How many pounds of sugar do you eat a year?
3. Can you name a time when you were hurt by something you did wrong?

We need to be careful so we don't hurt ourselves.

seventeen

The Subway System

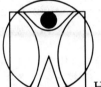 Have you ever ridden in a subway? Large cities such as New York City, Washington, D.C., and other cities throughout the world have subways. In subways. trains travel quickly, taking people underground to different parts of the city.

A person walking the streets in one of these cities cannot see the trains because they are hidden. But still the trains keep doing their job.

The human body has a tiny subway system. It is not visible, but yet it keeps doing its job. It is called the capillary system. It works hard to carry blood and small pieces of waste to and from various cells.

Perhaps you have heard about arteries and veins. Both of them carry blood. The capillaries look like a fine fishnet connected to the arteries and veins.

Capillaries are much, much thinner than a human hair. It would take fifty capillaries to be as thick as one hair. The capillary walls are so thin that food and oxygen can pass through them easily. With special equipment a scientist can see through a capillary.

Since capillaries are so small blood cells actually have to bend down to fit through. It takes thousands of tiny blood cells to fill up even an inch of capillary.

This subway system is so small it can be studied only with a strong microscope.

The human body contains billions of these little capillaries. If the capillaries in an adult's body could be removed and placed end to end, they would reach all the way around the earth— maybe twice.

Not all of our capillaries are working at once. Some will rest while others are carrying blood. Then, suddenly you need to lift something with your right arm, and blood quickly packs into the resting capillaries. But suppose you have to grab something with your left arm. In a wink the blood fills the capillaries in that arm also.

Our capillaries are more than just a subway system. The blood cells do all their work in these tiny tubes. Our blood gives off oxygen through its walls because they are so thin. It also picks up carbon dioxide the same way.

We can't see the subways, heart pumps, disease fighters and blood makers working in our body. They go about their job quietly and most of the time they work excellently.

Just because we can't see capillaries, however, doesn't mean that they are missing. They are invisible to us but still very real. The fact that we are still alive proves they are there.

The same thing is true of God. We have never seen Him, but He goes on working. He watches over our lives, listens to us, and acts directly when He needs to. We don't have to see God to know He is on the job.

"Glory and honor to God forever and ever. He is the King of the ages, the unseen one who never dies; he alone is God, and full of wisdom. Amen" (1 Tim. 1:17, TLB).

1. How many capillaries make the thickness of one hair?
2. What is a capillary?
3. How do you know God is real?

Faith in God is believing in Someone we do not see.

eighteen

A Frightening Word

 Cancer is a word we hear often, and it never sounds pleasant. Cancer is a terrible disease which hurts many people all around us. Even though we hear about it so often, most of us know very little about what causes it.

You probably know at least one person who has cancer. Every year one million people get the disease and almost 400,000 die from it. Only heart disease kills more people. For every five people who die this year, one of them will die from cancer.

These are just numbers, but let's compare them. Every year thousands of people are killed in automobile accidents. However, eight times as many people die yearly from cancer as from cars.

In spite of these high numbers, many people who get cancer do not die. Those who find it early have the best chance of being cured. We are surrounded by many friends and relatives who have had cancer and are now living happy, healthy lives. Many mothers and fathers have received treatment for the disease and are back with their children again.

Two of the most common types of cancer are skin and lung cancer. Skin cancer is often cured—especially if found early.

Among men lung cancer happens more often. However, there seems to be an increase in lung cancer among women. Many scientists believe that lung cancer often is connected with smoking cigarettes.

The United States Surgeon General says the average smoker is ten times more likely to get lung cancer than the nonsmoker. The heavy smoker is twenty times more likely. This will take years to develop, but the risk seems great.

Does cigarette smoking cause cancer? Does smoking make it easier for cancer to grow? Either way smoking does seem to make the situation worse. Many who smoke will never get cancer. But they are taking a great risk.

What is cancer? It is a growth of unusual cells. If these cells grow slowly and do not destroy other cells and tissue, it may be of little trouble. Other growths move faster and as they reach out they destroy tissues and cut off the blood supply.

When these cells move, choke and destroy, many other damages are done to the body. If they are not stopped, they may do enough harm to kill a person.

In the past other diseases have existed which have killed huge numbers of people. Smallpox was a feared word because of the many thousands it killed. Today smallpox is under control in most countries and we are free to live without fear of it.

Someday we hope to see a cure for cancer. We need to pray for the scientists who are working hard to find an answer. Maybe there is a young person who will train himself, study and someday find an answer.

God cannot be happy with this death and destruction. He wants us to be as healthy as possible.

"Dear friend, I am praying that all is well with you and that your body is as healthy as I know your soul is" (3 John 2, TLB).

1. How many people get cancer each year?
2. What is cancer?
3. Do you think it would help to pray for an answer to cancer?

Show scientists how to do the impossible.

nineteen

Growing Tall or Short

 How tall are you going to be? Every child asks himself this sooner or later. Parents often try to guess how big their children will get. Sometimes they make marks on a wall and keep careful records of the growth.

A child grows fastest during the first year after birth. During this time he stretches out possibly ten inches longer.

There are a few times when we "jump up" in life. Relatives who haven't seen us for a while talk about how much we have grown.

There is an old theory that says we can know how tall a person will be by measuring him at two years of age. This theory claims that a child is half his adult height by the time he is two years old. There may be some truth to this, but don't be too sure. Bodies can surprise all of us.

The height of a child's parents helps determine how tall or short the child will be. If both parents are tall, the child will probably be tall. Children with two short parents are usually short. When one parent is short and the other parent is tall, the child may grow either way. This can vary, however. Sometimes short parents have a tall child.

Children don't usually notice much difference in their size until somewhere between 9 and 13 years of age. This is the time when many "jump up." At this time many girls become taller than the boys. Often both the boys and girls feel odd about the differences in their height. But don't worry! By 16 many of the boys catch up.

This is the way it happens for many but not for all. Some people are short until their teenage years and then "jump up." Others become tall early and then slow down or stop.

Many of us worry about our height, but there is little we can do about it either way. The best thing we can do is eat the right foods, get the correct exercise and a good night's rest. When we stay healthy we help our growth the best way we can.

Some people not only don't grow tall but they stay extremely short. Usually those who stay around four feet tall or those who stretch to seven feet or more have a problem with their pituitary gland. This important part of the body is located at the bottom of our brain. When it doesn't work properly our size may be different from others.

How tall or short a person may be has nothing to do with how valuable he is. Some of the nicest people will never reach five feet tall. Often the best friends are well over six feet. The most important thing is not our size but what we are like.

Whether a person is small or tall doesn't really matter to God. He loves us and invites us into His family.

"Of a truth I perceive that God is no respecter of persons" (Acts 10:34, KJV).

1. What makes you grow seven feet tall or over?
2. Are we all the same size?
3. Does God love all of us the same?

Thanks for loving me just the way I am.

twenty

No More Storks

There was a time when many parents told their children that babies were brought by storks. The child would picture a long-winged, big-beaked bird flying to their house with a baby wrapped in a big diaper and tied to the stork's bill.

Now we believe in telling children exactly where they come from. We discuss the mother's womb and what life was like before the child was born.

Ten days after the egg and sperm come together in the womb, the egg will hold onto the wall of the womb. The egg will feed from this wall.

At the age of two weeks the tiny body will begin to grow. It pushes out and becomes longer.

After three weeks the small dot of a heart and lungs begins. Two little marks show where the eyes will be.

During the fourth week more organs start showing up. A speck of a brain can be seen. The head can now be seen to take some shape. Blood circulation has now started to do its work.

The fifth week brings tiny buds which will become arms and legs. A small tongue starts to form.

Little toes and fingers come into view around the sixth week. Different parts of the brain can be noticed.

During the eighth week bones have begun to take shape. Tiny teeth can be seen. Ears have moved out on the head. It is easy to recognize this form as being human even though it is only two months old.

The third month brings its vocal cords into good shape. The skull starts to become firm. At this time the child is called a fetus.

In the fourth month the brain develops more. The fifth month gives a workable windpipe. Eyebrows, fingerprints and footprints are all in place during the sixth month.

The special month is number seven. If absolutely necessary, a baby might survive if it is born now. Its eyelids could open if it suddenly found itself outside the mother.

The ninth month is the best. When a fetus can stay in the mother this long it has a great chance to become a healthy child.

Many times we think of a tiny body as just being a strange little blob inside the mother. This is far from the fact. God has made us so that each week our small fetus does another amazing thing. We can thank God for a body which is marvelously made.

"You made all the delicate, inner parts of my body, and knit them together in my mother's womb. Thank you for making me so wonderfully complex! It is amazing to think about. Your workmanship is marvelous—and how well I know it" (Ps. 139:13-14, TLB).

1. What is a fetus?
2. In what week do toes and fingers show up?
3. At what age are some fetuses more likely to live?

Our bodies are a Master plan.

twenty-one

Broken Bones

My son broke his collarbone three times. Each time it was painful but it healed well. He had to wear an arm sling for two of the breaks but none for the third.

Another name for a broken bone is a fracture. Most people have one sooner or later. A few fractures are not much trouble and the person goes on with his normal life. Some are so bad the individual has to stay in bed for weeks.

God has given us strong bodies and bones which heal well. Our bones are not like lifeless steel rods. Bones are more like tree branches. While they are attached to the tree they are living.

Many broken bones would heal without a doctor's help. If the broken pieces are touching, they will probably grow back together. But the large part of the doctor's job is to make sure the bone grows straight. If the blood flow is open, it will take care of the healing.

A new material forms at the place of the break. This glue is called callus. My son did not break his collarbone three times in the same place. The area where it had healed was actually stronger than the rest of the bone. In many cases the place of the break will look like the rest of the bone in a short time.

Young bodies generally work better than old ones. One reason is because they heal better. A small child's bones want to bend. An older person's have too much calcium and break easier. This brittleness makes it more difficult for the bone to heal. This is why many grandparents are especially afraid of falling.

Sometimes surgery is needed to set the bone into place. If necessary a steel pin can be put in the bone to hold it correctly.

People can be like bones. We might get angry and break off a good friendship. Like a broken bone it often hurts.

If we care enough, most friendships—like bones—can be put back together. It is important to heal friendships before they become broken too seriously.

"Dear friends, since God loved us as much as that, we surely ought to love each other too" (1 John 4:11, TLB).

1. Do you have to have surgery to put a bone back into place?
2. What is the glue called that forms at a break?
3. When did you last "heal" a problem with a friend?

Friendships heal well if we give them a chance.

twenty-two

The Terrible Tapeworm

His name was Ernie and he had a strange habit. When he was in the kitchen he liked to grab a pinch of uncooked hamburger and eat it. If Ernie knew what kind of chance he was taking, he would probably quit it right away.

Many of us laugh and pretend we have a tapeworm. We might eat a big meal and say, "I'm just feeding my tapeworm." Actually, some people do have a tapeworm, and more than likely they got it from eating uncooked or improper meat.

Tapeworms like to live in animals. But then they are happy to live in fish, dogs or people. They have no eyes or ears so they aren't sure where they are.

Most people are not eager to get a tapeworm inside them. Though tiny they can grow to over 30 feet long. Tapeworms live off the partly digested food inside the animal or person.

They begin by laying an egg inside the animal. The egg hatches into a larva. When we buy meat, it might have this larva in it. This is nothing to worry about. If we cook the meat well, the larva is destroyed and can't possibly harm us.

But suppose someone were foolish enough to eat raw meat— like Ernie? If a tapeworm larva was in the meat, it would try to live inside the person. The person might feel weak because the tapeworm is eating some of his nourishment. The tapeworm is also giving off juices which could make the person feel sickly. Fortunately there are good medicines which can get rid of tapeworms.

Man has vegetables, fruits, milk and meat to eat and keep him healthy. If he is careful and uses them well, his body will work well. When he becomes foolish with these good things, he may hurt himself.

This is true of the things which go into our mouth, but the same is true of what goes into our ears. Every day we hear thousands of words. Some are fascinating. Some are helpful. Some are terrible.

Long ago a man named Job told us to be careful about the words we hear. Not everything is worth listening to. Some words only lead to trouble. Some words only hurt people. Many words aren't even true.

We don't eat meat unless it is cooked correctly. We shouldn't listen to words unless they are good, helpful and true.

"For the ear trieth words, as the mouth tasteth meat" (Job 34:3, KJV).

1. How long are tapeworms?
2. Where do they begin?
3. Can you think of words you wish you had not heard?

Some things are not worth listening to.

twenty-three

Healthy Milk

 If our body is to run well, it has to have the right types of fuel. You wouldn't try to run a car with syrup instead of gas. You wouldn't try to feed sand to a horse.

One of the best fuels for the human body is a big glass of cold milk. Most of us are used to drinking cows' milk. However, more people around the world drink goats' milk than cows' milk. In some countries they drink yaks' milk.

But why so much fuss over milk? Milk has many of the necessary foods our body needs.

Milk contains protein, fats and carbohydrates. In a young, growing body these nutrients can help the person get a healthy start. The same thing can be said for calcium and phosphorus. When you are developing bones and teeth, these two elements help tremendously.

When you are young a quart of milk every day isn't too much to drink. When you become an adult half this amount each day is sufficient.

Many years ago it was dangerous to drink milk. This drink used to be excellent for carrying and holding germs. Sometimes scarlet fever or diphtheria germs would get into the milk and hundreds of people would catch these diseases.

Perhaps someone working with the cows had had the disease. Or maybe one of the cows was sick. Today both the workers and the cows are checked carefully to make sure disease cannot happen.

A further step is taken to make sure that the milk is healthy. If you buy milk in cartons, read what is written on the carton. Look for two words: pasteurized and homogenized.

Milk is pasteurized to make sure there are no germs in it. There is no reason to worry about milk anymore, since most milk purchased in stores has been pasteurized.

Today milk is also homogenized. This is not done for health reasons, however. Homogenizing breaks the fat into smaller pieces and keeps the cream and milk mixed together. If milk isn't homogenized, the cream will form thickly at the top of the bottle or carton.

Soft drinks, coffee and tea can also be fun to drink. However, none of these will help make you as strong and healthy as milk will.

You will always be glad if you get your body off to a healthy start. You will enjoy life more when you feel well and are able to think clearly.

The same rule applies to the Christian's life. If a person starts his walk with Christ correctly, he will always be glad. The best way to begin with Christ is by knowing what the Bible says. It tells us about a fantastic Savior and how we can follow Him.

"As newborn babies, desire the sincere milk of the word, that ye may grow thereby" (1 Pet. 2:2, KJV).

1. What kind of milk do most people drink?
2. Why is milk pasteurized?
3. Why is the Bible important to us?

We get a good look at Christ in the Bible.

twenty-four

Why Are People Fat?

The answer to this question seems simple at first. The human body uses food like fuel. Gas, coal or electricity keep a furnace going. Food allows a body to stay healthy. If a person takes in more food than his body can "burn up," he will discover that the extra food becomes fat.

A fat or chubby person eats more than his body needs. Someone says if he wants to lose weight, he should eat less. This is basically true; however, we should remember that for some people losing weight is extremely difficult.

One out of four overweight people also has overweight parents. If both parents are heavy, in most cases the child will also be heavy. The eating habits built into this family must be changed not only in the child but also in the parents.

Sometimes people eat less food, expecting to lose weight, but do not succeed. They may be eating the wrong kinds of foods—the kinds that offer too much fuel for burning.

Whatever the situation may be, we must be careful never to tease overweight people. God loves them very much and wants to help them overcome both their "inside" problems and their "outside" problems.

If a person wants to lose weight, he will find there are two practical ways to do it. The first is to eat less. Most of us would become thinner if we cut down on food. The second step is to get more exercise. By moving our bodies we use the food and calories we have eaten. When they "burn up" by activity, they cannot become body fat.

Everybody has fat. The problem comes when we have too much. Fat will line the body, especially just under the skin. Fat will pile up around the kidneys. It will also lie around the heart. This added weight makes the heart and muscles work harder. Often we become tired easily. Many people with too much weight die earlier than those with the right amount.

God created several parts in the human body. We have a mind which gets better the more we use it. We have a spiritual side which grows when we learn more about God. And we have a body which houses our mind and spirit. Our body should not sit around getting fat and slow. A poorly kept body hurts our minds and our spirits.

"For bodily exercise profiteth little: but godliness is profitable unto all things, having promise of the life that now is, and of that which is to come" (1 Tim. 4:8, KJV).

1. What makes you fat?
2. What are two ways to lose weight?
3. How can we serve God by having a healthy body?

Keep us from letting our bodies become run-down.

twenty-five

The Bad-Tempered Organ

 "He is a hot-head. It must come from his spleen." That is what people used to think. If people saw someone becoming angry quickly, they thought it came from this part of his body.

There might be many causes for a bad temper, but we are sure the spleen isn't the reason.

Most of us have probably never heard of the spleen. It isn't the body's most publicized organ. Even doctors and scientists have trouble understanding it. The spleen sort of changes jobs. It is an important part of our body and yet it may not really be important at all.

This is where the confusion comes in: when we are first born the spleen's job is to make red blood cells and white blood cells. Immediately after birth it switches jobs. The spleen still makes white blood cells, but now it is destroying red blood cells.

Is it dangerous to have red blood cells destroyed? No. In fact it is helpful.

A red blood cell is good for about one month of service in the human body. After that the cells are useless. Our bone marrow is making plenty of new red cells. What will happen to the old ones? The spleen and liver work together to destroy around 10 million of them every second. It has to be done because 10 million new ones are entering the bloodstream every second.

The spleen is the graveyard for red blood cells.

What happens if this important organ stops working? Here is part of its mystery. The body seems to get along very well without the spleen. Other parts take over and do the job the spleen was supposed to do. If the spleen is removed in surgery, the bone marrow begins to produce more white cells at once.

The spleen is not a small organ. It is about the size of your fist. It is three to five inches long and weighs maybe one-fourth of a pound.

A spleen holds blood. Some scientists believe this works as an extra supply in case our body needs it. Others find this hard to believe.

Doctors and scientists know a great many things about the body. There are also many things they don't understand. The body is an amazing mystery. In the past 100 years God has allowed us to learn a tremendous amount about it.

Our body is able to create, build and heal itself. It is also capable of throwing off the old to make room for the new. The spleen plays an important role in keeping the body healthy by getting rid of what is no longer useful.

As we grow up we continue to sort out and get rid of many things in our lives. There are some habits we should drop. Perhaps you used to cry if you didn't get your way. Or maybe you broke things when you got angry. Now you are growing up and want to stop old and harmful habits.

"You are living a brand new kind of life that is continually learning more and more of what is right, and trying constantly to be more and more like Christ who created this new life within you" (Col. 3:10, TLB).

1. How large is the spleen?
2. What does a spleen do?
3. Name one habit you used to have.

Show me what I should get rid of.

twenty-six

Don't Yawn!

 Try not to yawn while you are reading this chapter. It is dangerous to even discuss this subject. The thought of yawning is enough to make most people do it. If we see someone yawn, we will probably copy them most of the time.

Now remember—don't yawn!

Yawning is almost impossible to control. You can tell yourself you refuse to yawn, but it won't do much good. Yawning is controlled by involuntary nerves. They normally do not listen to the person but do as they please.

There are several things which start someone yawning. The biggest problem is just being tired. Being bored will do the same thing. Usually we stretch our arms and legs while yawning.

In most cases our breathing has slowed down. There isn't enough oxygen getting into our lungs. If the room is not getting enough fresh air, this will help bring on the yawns.

Now remember—don't yawn!

If you begin to yawn you probably can't stop it. Maybe you will be able to keep your mouth closed (and maybe not). But this won't stop it. Your body muscles will still move and you will yawn inside.

Even animals yawn. Their muscles relax and their oxygen intake slows down.

The middle part of our brain seems to control our yawning. Whatever part of the brain it is, little can stop it. Why do we yawn when we see someone else do it? Is it because the sight reminds our body it is tired? That is a tough one to answer.

Now remember—don't yawn!

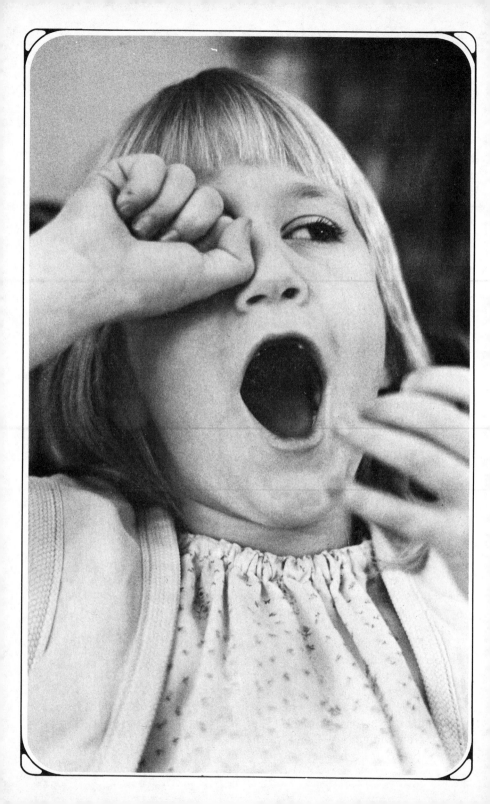

If you want to put an end to it, some things will help. Going to bed might be one idea. Another one is to walk outside and get some fresh air. The supply of oxygen might wake you up. A glass of cold water or washing your face might also help. If none of these things work, going to bed is possibly your only hope.

Thanks for not yawning.

All of us grow tired. No one has to be taught how to yawn. We all do it.

Can you think of one person who probably has never yawned? What about God? The Bible tells us He never grows tired. He never takes a nap or goes on vacation. He is always close by our side.

He never gets tired of watching over us. He never gets bored from listening to us. God is always alert and interested in us.

"Don't you yet understand? Don't you know by now that the everlasting God, the Creator of the farthest parts of the earth, never grows faint or weary? No one can fathom the depths of his understanding" (Isa. 40:28, TLB).

1. What is an involuntary nerve?
2. Why do you yawn?
3. When does God get tired?

Thanks for not yawning.

twenty-seven

What About Drugs?

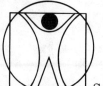

Some drugs are a big help. If a person has pain which will not stop, his doctor may give him drugs. These are medicines and need to be used carefully.

A few people cannot sleep night after night. Their doctor may order some pills to help them relax and go to sleep.

It is possible to buy a number of mild drugs without a doctor's order. They can be bought off the shelves in local drugstores. These drugs can be a great help to sick people. They can also be a terrible problem when they are used too often or too much at one time.

Doctors are concerned that we are using them more than we need to. In the United States we use over 10 billion pills every year just to help "pick us up." There are billions of others just to calm us down.

There are two long words to describe them. Amphetamines are supposed to pick us up and make us feel better. Barbiturates slow us down and help us relax.

Without a doctor's care it is easy to overuse these. Every time we have trouble getting started or slowing down, we might be tempted to take a few pills. Some are taking pills to get up and then to get down all in the same day.

If we use these drugs too often, our life could start to change. Instead of eating good food, getting healthy exercise or going to sleep at night, we let the drugs do it for us. They can be extremely dangerous.

Some people are "hooked" on these common drugs and pills. This means they can't get along without them. Sooner or later they may hurt their body or mind from the wrong use of drugs.

Once in a while we hear of someone who has died from too many drugs. Others die because they take drugs and drink too much alcohol at the same time. The mixture can become a type of poison.

Many others are being hurt physically and mentally from using "hard" drugs such as heroin and cocaine. These can also become "addictive." Addictive means that a person's body becomes hungry for the drug and he cannot get along without it.

There are many people "hooked" on drugs who wish they had never tried them. It is usually dumb to use drugs without a doctor's attention.

God wants us to take care of our bodies. He wants us to enjoy them. If we mess up our bodies by the wrong use of drugs, we could become terribly unhappy.

"No one hates his own body but lovingly cares for it, just as Christ cares for his body, the church, of which we are parts" (Eph. 5:29, 30, TLB).

1. What is an amphetamine?
2. What is a barbiturate?
3. Why does God care about your body?

Our bodies are too amazing to hurt them foolishly.

twenty-eight

Holes in Your Head

 If you want to insult someone, just tell him he's got holes in his head. Although it's unkind to say that to someone, it's a true statement. We all have several holes inside our head. They are called sinus cavities and they have a good purpose.

Another name for cavities is pockets. The pockets located around the nose are called nasal sinuses.

One group of sinuses is located just above our eyes. Another set is found behind the nose. A third group is found on each side of the nose. A fourth set is beside our cheekbones.

If there were no pockets, our head would become too heavy. Our neck would become tired and shoulders feel strained just from trying to keep our head up. Most of the time we would probably just rest our chin on our chest.

This isn't the only good use for sinuses. When we sing, these pockets allow us to have a pleasant sound. A guitar has a hollow case for the same reason. Without these cavities, singing would sound flat and dull.

Most of the time we don't pay attention to these pockets. They are just there. Each is lined with a soft liquid called mucus. When we catch a cold, these cavities let us know they are around.

During a cold the mucus will begin to fill up the pockets and overflow. They flow into the nose and we end up with a runny nose. After a time the cold goes away and the cavities go back to normal. A few people have trouble with too much fluid in the sinus pockets.

Colds aren't the only things which give us a "heavy" head. Sometimes we are troubled and our head hangs down like a gigantic stone. When the problem goes away, we feel like lifting up our head and smiling again.

Jesus Christ is a great head lifter. He helps people who are sad and discouraged. He gives them faith and hope. Pick up your head and smile—Jesus loves you.

"But Lord, you are my shield, my glory, and my only hope. You alone can lift my head, now bowed in shame" (Ps. 3:3, TLB).

1. What is one purpose of sinuses?
2. Show where one sinus is located.
3. What do you do when you feel sad?

Thanks for being a "head lifter."

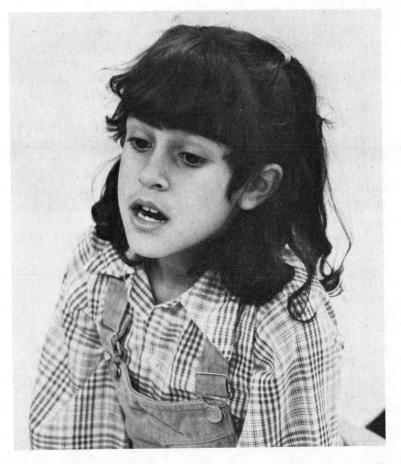

twenty-nine

Bacteria Isn't All Bad

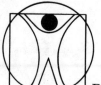

Bacteria has a bad name. Immediately most of us think about how harmful they can be. Maybe we picture tiny creatures crawling all over us making us sick. To many, the word bacteria means dirty.

The truth is most bacteria are not only safe but are even helpful. A few of them could give us mumps or measles but they are rare.

We have bacteria all over our body. They are small creatures which can be seen only under a magnifying glass. Thousands of them would fit into the dot over an i.

There is no way to get away from bacteria and still stay on earth. The closest anyone comes are the few people who must live in bubbles (a closed area free of germs). Their bodies cannot handle germs so they have to be protected.

When you walk outside you are immediately surrounded by bacteria. The rain washes them down onto your body. The winds whirl them up against your skin. If you sit on the ground, bacteria push onto you. They are alive on this book as you read it. You can't escape them. Right now they are moving around inside your body.

Some people have a terrible fear of bacteria. It is smart to stay clean, but some let their minds get carried away with worry. They think every little thing contains bacteria. Well, actually they are correct. However, there is no way to escape them. The cloth you use to wash off a table top contains thousands of bacteria.

Many bacteria are good for us. For instance, cheese is made from dairy products and the right mixture of bacteria. If you want one type of cheese, one type of bacteria is added. When you want another kind, you select a different bacteria.

The same thing is needed if you want to make cottage cheese. Vinegar is also made this way.

Human bodies need to be protected from harmful bacteria. That is why we wash our hands and brush our teeth. Scientists work hard to control bacteria. They want to learn how to control the bad ones and how to use the good ones.

Bacteria are so tiny they have to be studied carefully. By using thick microscopes scientists are learning more about the effects of bacteria on our lives. Their close attention will make our future much brighter.

Can you imagine God looking through a microscope? Underneath the glass is someone who looks exactly like you. Imagine God looking you over just that carefully. He cares about each small part of you. He knows far more about us than we ever will. God gives us His personal attention.

"O Lord, you have examined my heart and know everything about me" (Ps. 139:1, TLB).

1. Where can you find bacteria?
2. Give a good use for bacteria.
3. When are we alone?

Thanks for knowing more about us than we know about ourselves.

thirty

A Fascinating Food Sack

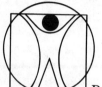 Put your hand on your stomach. Where do you think it is located? Most people will probably place their hand around their belly button or lower. The stomach is really higher up, just at the bottom of our rib cage off center to the left.

The stomach is a busy worker and does some amazing jobs. Most of the time it isn't large until we eat. Then it stretches like a balloon and can hold a big meal.

For three to five hours after each meal the human stomach works at full speed. Its biggest job is to break down the food into very small parts so that the body can use it.

Your stomach is lined with 35 million tiny glands. These small specks produce digestive juices which work on our food. We would really be in trouble without them. Some scientists believe crocodiles swallow rocks, bottles and even bracelets to help break up their food. Digestive juices work much better.

The juices we have are extremely strong. Sometime look at the food on your dinner plate and think of the job your stomach must do. It has to change meat, pickles, apples, pie, popcorn and pizza so that the body can use them.

In one 24-hour day the stomach must produce two to three quarts of gastric juices. Sometime look at a quart jar to see what a large amount this is.

The juices carry on a double job. Not only do they dissolve food, but they also fight germs and other bacteria. A few parasites live through this acid bath, but most harmful things are destroyed.

Juices as strong as these could become dangerous to the stomach itself if the inside wasn't protected. Our stomach is lined with a film called mucus. Too much gastric juice will give some people trouble. A bare place could begin to wear away in the lining and cause pain. The mucus does an excellent job for most of us.

When the stomach has finished its job, the processed food is pushed into our intestines. While in the intestines the nutrients or healthy parts of the food are sent into the rest of the body. The small intestine is 22 feet long in some people.

Fortunately we have strong bodies which handle almost any normal food. If we don't eat "odd" things, our stomachs and intestines will take good care of us.

Jesus Christ told us our biggest problems do not come from what we put into our bodies. Far more serious is what comes out of our mouths and minds. Some people worry all the time that they eat the right thing. Jesus told us to be more concerned over what we say.

"Your souls aren't harmed by what you eat, but by what you think and say" (Mark 7:15, 16, TLB).

1. How many tiny glands is your stomach lined with?
2. How long is the small intestine?
3. Why are words more important than food?

Help us guard what comes out of our mouths.

thirty-one

Will It Be a Boy or Girl?

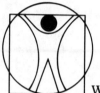

When you grow up, which would you like to have—a boy or a girl? Do you imagine two little girls or two boys sitting on your lap? Maybe you picture one of each.

There once was a time when parents wanted more boys than girls. This is still true in a few countries. Girls were raised in order to give them away in marriage. The boys would be kept to take over the farm or business. Today things are different. Parents realize that girls and boys are equally important.

What determines whether a girl or a boy is born? Why is a boy born one time and a girl the next? Sometimes a boy and a girl are born at the same time.

The very second a female egg and a male sperm come together inside the mother, the sex of the baby is settled. Inside, the egg and the sperm are tiny parts called chromosomes. Chromosomes make up the sex of the child.

Mothers always have X chromosomes. However, the father can have either X or Y chromosomes.

If a father's X chromosome matches up with the mother, the baby will be a girl. But if a father's Y chromosomes connect with the mother's X chromosomes, the baby will be a boy.

Neither the father nor the mother has any control over this. The father's cells throw off either an X or Y chromosome. The one left determines the sex of the child.

Inside the chromosomes are tiny genes. The genes help decide our appearance. We receive blue or brown eyes depending on what kind of genes have their way. Healthy genes will help a great deal in forming a healthy child.

The fact is, girls are not made from sugar and spice and everything nice. They are created from X chromosomes. Boys are not made from frogs and snails and puppy dog tails. They come from X and Y chromosomes.

Both boys and girls are equally important. Both can be extremely nice. Both can be terribly bad. They can make their parents proud and happy. They can be helpful and kind. They can't choose if they want to be a girl or a boy, but they can decide whether to be considerate or mean.

We can't choose if we are white, brown, black, or any other race. We can't choose if we are short or tall. But we can choose if we want to follow Jesus Christ or ignore Him. Those who choose to ignore Him are heading for tremendous troubles.

"Choose ye this day whom ye will serve" (Josh. 24:15, KJV).

1. What chromosomes produce a boy?
2. Who are most important—girls or boys?
3. Have you decided to become a Christian?

I am glad you made me what I am.

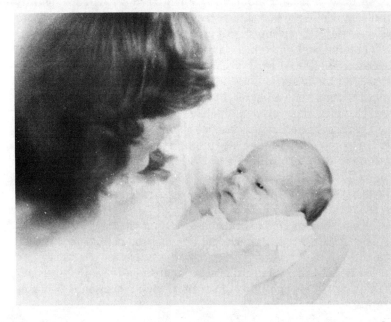

thirty-two

Fresh Breath

 If you watch the commercials on television, you might think everyone has "bad" breath. People are buying breath mints, deodorants and mouthwashes. There is no doubt that sometimes we need these.

A hundred years ago people probably did not need them, since people did not live close and others did not notice breath as much.

In most cases our mouth will smell fresh if it is both healthy and clean. When we brush our teeth well and rinse our mouth, we usually don't have much difficulty.

Imagine that you don't clean your mouth after a meal. When bacteria is allowed to stay there, it will begin to rot or decompose. As this bacteria changes it gives off an odor. When people stand close to you they might be able to smell the rotting bacteria. Sometimes you can smell it yourself.

If our teeth and mouth are not cleaned regularly, the problem will become worse. After a while our teeth will begin to decay. Our decaying teeth will then also add to the odor. If our gums become "sick," they too will smell badly. Many children have a pleasant smell to their breath. This is probably because their parents insist on a clean mouth.

When we eat, smoke or drink anything with a strong odor, it is usually left on our breath. Onions may be delicious, but they leave a strong smell.

Sometimes a stuffed-up nose will cause bad breath. Air is unable to pass through our mouth properly and an odor becomes trapped.

"Bad" breath can also be caused by poor health. A person can be sick and the odor from his stomach or other parts will come up into his mouth.

Almost everyone likes to be around other people. It is more pleasant when everyone has "fresh" breath. The best way to keep it nice is to clean our mouth thoroughly. If you need more help a small amount of salt mixed with water might work. When more help than this is needed some of the mouthwashes advertised on television might be what you want.

A mouth can be a healthy, clean, fresh part of our body. It can also be a rotting, smelly, unpleasant place. For most of us it all depends on what we want to make it.

We are able to control what goes into our mouth and what comes out. Sometimes we send out kind words. They pick people up and make them feel good. Other times we say ugly things, hoping to make someone feel badly. The choice is always up to us. We will be happier with ourselves if we say "fresh" and helpful words.

"And so blessing and cursing come pouring out of the same mouth. Dear brothers, surely this is not right" (James 3:10, TLB).

1. What causes "bad" breath?
2. What causes "fresh" breath?
3. Name one way we use our mouth in an ugly way.

Help me keep my mouth clean.

thirty-three

New Eyes

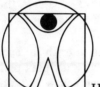 Hold up a pop bottle to your eye and try to see the room through it. You can probably make out some furniture and people, but it is difficult. Everything looks cloudy and it is a strain to see.

Now you have some idea of what it is like to have a poor cornea. The cornea is a clear piece of tissue which covers the eye. If something goes wrong with the cornea, it is like looking through a dirty window. For some, the window is so dirty they really can't see well enough to lead an ordinary life.

Until recently a scarred or cloudy cornea meant a limited life. The harder it became to see, the more the person had to draw back, do less and go less places. After a great deal of study doctors have found a way to remove the cornea from someone who has just died and attach it to the eye of a living person. This is a tremendous miracle because it allows thousands of people to see again.

This is often called an eye transplant, but this isn't really what happens. Only the front cornea or window of the eye is used.

If someone wants to leave his cornea after death, the job is simple. The person leaving it doesn't even have to have good eyesight. I wear thick glasses because I can't see things far away. But if I give my cornea away, the person getting it will not have my eyesight. The person will have his own eyesight but will use my "windows."

Corneal transplants do not work for everyone, but they do for thousands. Many people are waiting for a new cornea and cannot live a full life until they get one or two. There are now "eye banks" to help get corneas to the right people in time. The cornea must be removed soon after death. It is then sent immediately to a bank and assigned to someone who needs it.

Few things are as important as seeing. If we try going ten minutes with our eyes closed, we know how much we miss sight. With a little help we can see much more. Microscopes allow us to see tiny pieces our normal eyes miss. Telescopes let us look at stars too far away to see.

No matter what our vision, none of us has seen God. Jesus Christ said He could help us. He told us if we will look at Him, we will see God the Father. The more we know about Jesus the more we know about God.

"Anyone who has seen me has seen the Father" (John 14:9, TLB).

1. What is a cornea?
2. Does a person have the same eyesight as the one who gave him a cornea?
3. How can we "see" Jesus Christ?

Thanks for letting us see God in Jesus Christ.

thirty-four
Miserable Burns

 "Ouch!" Brent dropped the pan, spilling water all over the kitchen floor. Someone had left part of the handle over the flame and it became hot. It didn't take Brent a full second to let go.

Brent's burned fingers will hurt for a short time, but nothing serious has happened. It is a normal burn which most of us have had at one time or another.

For this type of burn the skin proves plenty tough. Brent's fingers will probably turn red. Maybe they will even puff up. Brent is fortunate, though, because the skin was not destroyed and no blister formed. He received a first-degree burn.

There are half a dozen ways to get this type of burn. A slight case of sunburn or hot water from the faucet are just two of the causes.

It isn't hard for this burn to heal. There will probably be no mark left.

What happens if the burn is worse? Suppose you stay out in the sun too long or the pan is too hot? In this case the skin may burn deeply. The top layer of skin may be destroyed and fluids may run from the tissues. A blister will probably form on the burn.

Many doctors will tell us not to break this blister. It is filled with valuable liquid which fights germs. Do not allow those liquids to escape lest the healing be more difficult.

This is called a second-degree burn. Sometimes this type of burn can make you sick. One summer my legs were burned badly on the first day at the beach. I was sick for days and sometimes in considerable pain. My burn healed without leaving marks.

A third-degree burn does a great deal of damage. It might burn through the entire thickness of skin and destroy other parts. This type of burn could be so serious as to need new skin put on the wound. Moving skin from one part of the body to another is called grafting. It can be taken from another part of the person's own body or be taken from someone else's body.

Fire is a gigantic help. It can warm bodies and prepare food. If it isn't handled correctly, however, fire can also destroy houses and ruin our skin.

This is true of many things. The words we use can go either way too. We can say something nice about a brother or sister and make them feel great. We can tease and bug them and make them feel terrible. Some people even lie about each other and hurt them badly.

Lips are like fire. They can help or they can hurt.

"An ungodly man diggeth up evil: and in his lips there is as a burning fire" (Prov. 16:27, KJV).

1. What is a second-degree burn?
2. What is under a blister?
3. Has anyone ever hurt you by talking about you? Have you ever hurt someone else by talking about him?

Control my lips as we control a fire.

thirty-five

Food Has to Change

 When you eat a piece of cake it has to change. That light, fluffy inside with the chocolate icing tastes great on its way to your stomach. But by the time it gets to your stomach that cake had better begin to change if it is going to be good for you.

The pancreas is an important organ whose job it is to change that chocolate cake. Maybe you have never heard of the pancreas before. It isn't as well known as the heart or brain. But without a healthy pancreas, life will become difficult.

The pancreas is hiding just behind your stomach. It is a fairly long, slender organ.

When the chocolate cake starts its trip through your body, the pancreas begins its work at once. The sugars and other carbohydrates have to be treated immediately. Your body can't accept these unless they are changed.

The pancreas makes a chemical called insulin. It is this insulin which changes the sugars, making them ready to travel throughout the system.

Maybe you have a relative who is called a diabetic. There are many of them. He may be a diabetic because his pancreas does not produce enough insulin. This can happen to adults or small children.

If the pancreas does not make enough insulin, the person needs help. He must get insulin and put it into his body. This is the only way he can stay healthy.

This happens often. There are probably some students in your school who are diabetics. Before insulin became available as a medicine, many diabetics died. Today insulin is made either from special chemicals or taken from animals.

When the insulin from the pancreas fails to change our food into usable form, our body suffers.

Change is an important part of life. We would not have cars if we could not change minerals into metals. We would not have clothing if we could not change cotton and other material into cloth.

God is in the business of change. Some caterpillars change into butterflies, and tadpoles change into frogs. He changes mountain snow into beautiful streams.

He is also interested in changing people. Some people have led mean lives and then God changed them. Others were lonely and had no reason to live. God gave them purpose. Some felt far away from God and then He introduced himself.

There may be some things you would like to change in your life. God would like to help you make that change.

"When someone becomes a Christian he becomes a brand new person inside. He is not the same any more. A new life has begun!" (2 Cor. 5:17, TLB).

1. Where is your pancreas?
2. What is insulin?
3. Can you name someone whom God has changed?

In Christ we are different from what we were yesterday.

thirty-six

God's Unusual Gift

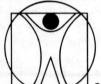 If you could have anything you wanted, what would it be? Maybe a boat or a snowmobile or a minibike, or a trip to Disneyland. Most of us probably have our own little list.

When God was giving gifts to people, He gave us an odd one. It is probably the last one we would have asked for. God gave us the gift of pain.

If you think this is strange, try to imagine yourself without the ability to feel pain. There are some who live without any pain in their arm or leg. Some people with leprosy cannot feel pain in one or more limbs.

Since they cannot know pain, life is dangerous. Sometimes they accidentally cut off a finger. Since they cannot feel pain, they don't realize they have cut their skin so they cut on through.

Maybe they are standing beside a fire and their sock catches on fire. Their foot could become seriously burned before they know what has happened.

A Christian doctor has tried to help lepers who cannot feel pain. He worked hard at trying to make tiny nerve cells. He wanted to place these cells into the person's hands and feet. Finally, the doctor had to give up. He could find no way to make this important cell which God originally created.

Many people are in too much pain. They need medicines or whatever means possible to reduce their suffering. However, the removal of all pain would be terribly dangerous.

What would happen if our appendix could not give off pain? It could become infected and start to swell up. We would think everything was all right. Finally the appendix could blow up and throw poison throughout our system. God thought of a better plan and gave us pain.

Not only is pain a warning but it also helps us heal. Suppose you sprain your ankle. Each time you step on it a sharp pain shoots through your body. The pain says, "Get off this foot so it can heal." Otherwise it could get worse and start to cripple us.

God did not decide to place a few cells here and a few cells there. No part of our body can be hurt without feeling pain. One inch on your arm, knee or hands has thousands of tiny cells—each one ready to announce any pain which arrives.

We don't understand everything God does. Sometimes we think: "I wonder why God doesn't do this or that." It is hard to say. But the actions of God are often mysteries. We might not do it His way, but then we are wrong many times. Most of us probably would not have thought to create pain.

Why God sent His Son is a mystery to many. But we are glad He did.

"Withal praying also for us, that God would open unto us a door of utterance to speak the mystery of Christ, for which I am also in bonds" (Col. 4:3, KJV).

1. Why do we have pain?
2. What might happen to our appendix without pain?
3. Why did God send His Son?

Life is filled with surprising gifts.

thirty-seven

What Causes Wrinkles?

 Touch the skin on your cheeks. It feels soft and bouncy. A man's skin is sometimes more firm than a woman's, but both are soft.

This "bouncy" touch is caused by a layer of fat just under our skin. Some have more fat than others, but all of us have a certain amount. If we start to get fat, this layer gets much larger. Sometimes the layer becomes so big it stretches the skin and makes marks or lines under the arms or on the legs.

When we are young our skin has plenty of oil to keep it healthy looking. During our early teens we might get too much oil for a while. When we grow old our body doesn't produce oil as well and our skin begins to look dry. People who have to work long hours in the sun and wind have their skin dry out faster.

As we grow older most of us are going to collect wrinkles. The layer of fat starts to weaken. It doesn't hold up as well and sometimes begins to break down. Our skin no longer has as much area to cover, and we really end up with too much skin. This is why people who stay fat have less wrinkles.

A few people get wrinkles before they are very old. Maybe their layer of fat becomes smaller earlier for some reason. Those who frown or squint a great deal cause their face to wrinkle too soon.

Once in a while children will laugh at people who have wrinkles. We forget what wrinkles mean. A person who is getting older has experience. He has seen a lot in life and learned many things. Older people make good counselors. God can use them to give excellent advice to young people. All of us could be kept from trouble if we stopped to ask the opinion of an older person. He could be a big help.

"The glory of young men is their strength; of old men, their experience" (Prov. 20:29, TLB).

1. What makes you get wrinkles?
2. Why doesn't your skin get wrinkled when you're ten?
3. Can you name an older person you enjoy being with?

Help us learn from people with wrinkles.

thirty-eight

The Embarrassing Burp

 It isn't the type of thing we usually talk about. Burping or belching even sounds like a funny or silly thing. Sometimes it is funny, but for most of us it is embarrassing.

Burping isn't considered rude everywhere. Among some people it is encouraged. They think of it as a sign that the food was appreciated and the guest is relaxed.

For most of us, however, burping remains a strange noise which comes roaring out of the throat. Children often like to make up the sound and pretend they are burping. This usually gets parents and teachers upset.

What causes us to burp? There are several reasons—some of them good and some not so good.

In young people the most common cause is poor eating habits. Instead of eating slowly and chewing thoroughly, they often gulp their food down. When they do this, they swallow a large amount of air. As this air begins to fill us up it tries to find some way to escape. Finally, it will push its way up and cause a loud burp.

Gulping food isn't good for us. Chewing food is an important part of our digestive system. If we fail to chew properly, we make our stomach juices work harder.

This is also a problem with people who do not have good teeth. They can't chew well and so they swallow large pieces of food and air.

How it goes down isn't the entire problem. Sometimes it is a question of what goes down. There are some soft drinks which are filled with gases. If you ever shook up a bottle, you could see the fizz. The body can hardly wait to chase this gas out again.

The problem may become a little more serious for adults. For some there is difficulty in the stomach. It doesn't handle the food correctly and gases are allowed to build up from the food itself.

Many adults have sensitive stomachs. They can't eat all the things young people can. Greasy or fried food, spices, pizza, cold drinks, too much liquid and many more can cause gas to build up and make the adult terribly uncomfortable.

What type of adult we will be depends greatly on what kind of young people we are. If we eat, sleep and exercise properly, our body will remain strong for many years. If we mistreat it, eat only junk food and don't care about our health, we may pay for it— sooner than we think.

"Don't let the excitement of being young cause you to forget about your Creator. Honor him in your youth before the evil years come—when you'll no longer enjoy living. It will be too late then to try to remember him, when the sun and light and moon and stars are dim to your old eyes, and there is no silver lining left among your clouds. For there will come a time when your limbs will tremble with age, and your strong legs will become weak, and your teeth will be too few to do their work, and there will be blindness too" (Ecc. 12:1-3, TLB).

1. What causes burping?
2. Why is chewing important for all ages?
3. Why are your habits as a youth important for your life as an adult?

Help us develop habits for a lifetime.

thirty-nine

Keep Your Balance

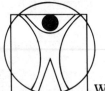Watch a football player race across a field. He sidesteps one person and stays on his feet. Another player tries a tackle, but he pulls away and refuses to go down. He is an excellent player because of his size and speed, but especially because of his balance. How can he stay on his feet so well?

Human beings are amazing. They are created with many special parts, but none more fascinating than the ability to keep balance.

The little machines which help us stay up are not found in our legs, arms or eyes. They are three tiny organs called canals located in our head. Each one is round and connected to strings of nerves.

Each canal is shaped like a small ball. Inside there is liquid and tiny fibers which are pushed together like straw on a broom.

Pretend you are walking on a log. Trying to keep your balance you begin leaning far to your left. This causes the liquid in your small canals and the fibers to move also. Immediately a message is sent to your brain, "You are off balance." The brain in turn gets the information to the rest of your body, "Straighten up." In a flash your arms, legs and muscles go to work to balance you. If you haven't gone too far too quickly, your balance system will rescue you.

This fast information from the canals, to the brain, to the muscles must be quick and correct. It not only has to say, "You are falling," it also has to tell which direction. "You are falling backward," "You are falling to the left and forward," or whichever direction. It is all part of our big computer and all parts work together.

In a few people the canal fluid moves too easily. They may get dizzy quickly or car sick often. Some people have serious trouble in this area and fall down often.

We are fortunate our balance canals work without being told to. If they didn't we couldn't skip, run, or walk a log without telling each leg and arm exactly what to do.

Most of life is the same way. We live without worrying because usually we are happy. But suddenly we are tempted to do something wrong. It sounds interesting, maybe even fun. Our conscience tells us to quickly catch ourselves or else we will fall. Keep your balance in life or you could do something you will be sorry for.

Christians need to be careful how they walk—it's easy to lose our balance and sin.

"So be careful. If you are thinking, 'Oh, I would never behave like that'—let this be a warning to you. For you too may fall into sin" (1 Cor. 10:12, TLB).

1. What is each canal shaped like?
2. How many balance organs are in our head?
3. Name two easy ways to "fall" and sin.

I need to live a balanced life.

forty
Ugly Bruises

 If someone told you you had a contusion, you would probably give him a funny look. If the same person said you had a bruise, you would understand. A contusion is simply a longer word for a bruise.

People collect bruises all the time. Children get them while playing games or climbing trees. Parents get bruises by smashing their thumb while hammering. The elderly get bruises by bumping against furniture or falling down.

There aren't many good-looking bruises. Most of them are ugly. Many are painful. And a few are dangerous.

One of the easiest ways to get a bruise is by getting a black eye. A person doesn't have to be in a fight, however, to collect a black eye. A three-year-old boy fell down and hit his forehead just between the eyes. The next day both of his eyes had large black and blue marks under them. For weeks people stared at him and wondered what had happened.

What usually happens is that the hit or blow breaks the thin blood vessels. Since the skin is not broken open the body cannot bleed outside, so it bleeds inside. The tissues around the vessel are also smashed down.

The blood, looking for a place to go, pours out into these tissues. When the tissues receive the blood, swelling starts immediately. The blood makes the area a dark black and blue.

Bruises occur easily around the eyes. One reason is because the tissue in this area is especially soft.

A bruise on the finger tip can be very painful because of the small area. Blood comes rushing out but has little room. This is especially true if it is near the fingernail. Since it has trouble moving, pressure builds up and causes pain.

The body bruises because something violent has happened to it. Blood vessels and tissue have been broken and the body is left suffering.

The Bible tells us about the bruises on the body of Jesus Christ. His body was hit and smashed. He was injured by the people who hated Him.

Why did the Son of God let people hurt Him? He volunteered to die in order to pay for our sins. When we have done something wrong, we can't erase it but Jesus Christ can.

You and I are given the forgiveness of God because Christ has erased our sins.

"But he was wounded and bruised for our sins. He was chastised that we might have peace; he was lashed—and we were healed" (Isa. 53:5, TLB).

1. What causes a bruise?
2. Why does the eye area bruise easily?
3. Why was Jesus Christ bruised?

My sins are paid for.

forty-one

Making Fun of People

There is a man who doesn't have any toes on one foot. He refused to let this stop him and he became a kicker on a professional football team. There is another person who is missing one leg so he had a special one made. He kicks for a college football team. There are some people who cannot walk at all and have to sit in a wheelchair. They started a basketball team for people in wheelchairs.

We often see people who are different from us. Some can't walk right and some can't see. Others have problems with their minds and can't think as well as we do. But they are still people and God loves them.

Most of us have some small handicap. Some of us are short and need to use a ladder. Others try hard to become outstanding athletes but never will make it. Some would like to learn mathematics quickly but instead it comes slowly. These may or may not be big things, but all of us are slow at something.

When we see someone who can't do what we can, we are sometimes nasty. Maybe we laugh at him or tell jokes behind his back. Instead of loving him we pick on his differences. We seem to forget that all of us are loved by God.

One of the common handicaps we see is a condition called mongolism. This person looks different because his mind and body were changed before birth. It is called mongolism because the eyes and other facial features make him look a little Asian.

This person was born with a limited mind. He can't learn or think half as well as you can. His mind will always be that of a small child. Because it happened before birth, not much can be done to help the mongoloid person.

If we took time to get to know him, we would find him pleasant, loving and easy to get along with. Because we don't understand the mongoloid person, we usually stay away or make fun of him.

People with this handicap often have poor health. They catch colds easily or get ear infections. It is easier for them to have heart trouble.

Mongoloids and all other handicapped people need the love of real Christians. Jesus loved the leper, short Zacchaeus, blind people, and a lame man who couldn't walk. Anyone can tease and make fun. It takes someone special to love people who are different.

"Jesus was moved with pity for them and touched their eyes. And instantly they could see, and followed him" (Matt. 20:34, TLB).

1. What do some people in wheelchairs do in sports?
2. What is one common handicap?
3. How did Jesus feel about the handicapped?

Help us to understand people who are different.

forty-two

What Are You Made Of?

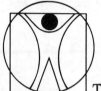 The answer to this one sounds easy. We are made of bones and skin and hair and teeth. It looks that way but actually we are made up of little cells too small for the human eye to see.

What makes a beach? Tiny grains of sand. One grain of sand doesn't amount to much. But if we put billions of them together we have a long, beautiful beach.

If we had a strong enough microscope, we could see the cells which make up our body. They are so small that over 1,000 could be placed inside one half an inch.

As you grow up, your body will increase its number of cells. Once you become an adult your number will stay the same. If you gain weight or lose it, your cell count does not change. You simply gain fat but not cells.

Don't try to count your cells. You have more than thousands. More than millions of cells. More than billions. There are at least trillions of cells in your body.

What does a cell look like? They come in just about every shape you could imagine. One may look like a starfish. The next one will look like a slice of bread. The third one will look like a worm. The fourth one will look like a fried egg.

They even change their shape. It depends on where they are in your body, and what they are doing at the time.

Different ones are in charge of special jobs just as in many homes. One cell has a paper route. Another cell takes out the trash. Some cells vacuum the living room. One cell goes to school. Another cell goes off to a job.

In your body one group of cells is in charge of keeping your bones strong. A second type of cell keeps your muscles strong and quick. A third group acts as messengers. Their job is to send signals rapidly around your body.

It is a good thing that cells stay with their friends. The muscle cells don't have an argument with each other, and forty of them move over to the nerve cells. Six bone cells don't get mad and go to live with the brain cells. If they did, our body would soon become an unorganized mess.

Imagine a muscle cell saying, "I'm tired of all this work. Nobody likes me here. I'm going to leave and join the liver cells."

Your body would not be able to work for very long. Your leg wouldn't work because it would be filled with brain cells.

We can be glad our cells stick together. They are just like good friends who help each other.

There is one friend who stays closer than any other. He doesn't get upset and walk away. His name is Jesus Christ. He comes into your life and becomes a part of you.

"There are 'friends' who pretend to be friends, but there is a friend who sticks closer than a brother" (Prov. 18:24, TLB).

1. How big is a cell?
2. How many cells do you have?
3. How does Jesus come into your life? (What do your parents think?)

Thank you for being with me day after day.

forty-three

The Ocean Inside

 How much of the earth is water? Around 70%. This means there is twice as much water on the earth as dry land. But this is only the beginning. The fruits, vegetables, animals and people around us are mostly water also.

A watermelon comes to mind right away. It is 99% water. Cucumbers have the same amount.

What about people? How much of your body is water? Before you were born it was 97%. When you were a baby it ran around 80%. When you become an adult it will still be 60%. There is more water in your body than anything else.

Just the correct amount of water is necessary to keep the human machine healthy. If we have either too much or too little, we start to become sick.

Our body is made up of tiny parts called cells. These cells are too small to see without a microscope. Well over half of each cell is made up of just plain water. If the amount becomes low the body cannot work as well.

The same thing is true of our blood. It is almost entirely water. If the amount of water in our blood becomes low also, the body has to slow down.

All bodies are different. That is why we don't act, think or look alike. The same thing is true of water content. The person sitting next to you could be the same age and have 80% water. You might have only 65%.

Who has the most water—heavy or thin people? Usually it is the skinny person. Water and fat do not like to mix.

Drinking good amounts of water each day is necessary for each of us. During the day we lose around a pint of water just from breathing. We might also lose a pint from sweating. We lose water by going to the bathroom. This is a large supply of liquid and we have to replace it every day.

Water is always important, but you notice it more if you live in a dry land. Jesus Christ lived in a country which did not get much rain. In some parts of Israel they received only four inches each year. Their bodies needed water and so did their crops and animals.

One day Jesus stood talking to a woman at a well. She knew how important this water was. Jesus knew that the body became thirsty and so does the soul.

The woman offered Jesus water from the well. Jesus offered her "water" for her soul. She could know the Son of God and have peace inside. Jesus called himself "living water."

Take care of your body and keep it healthy. But don't forget your soul, or the real you. It becomes thirsty to meet God. We can meet Him in Jesus Christ.

"He replied, 'If you only knew what a wonderful gift God has for you, and who I am, you would ask me for some living water'" (John 4:10, TLB).

1. How much of a watermelon is water?
2. Why do you need water?
3. How is Jesus Christ "living water"?

Jesus Christ satisfies the real me.

forty-four

Body Tape

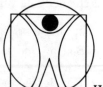 What is holding you together? Did you answer skin or muscles or a skeleton? All of these answers are correct. But how many of us have heard of a special tape which holds parts of us together. The name of the tape is cartilage.

Cartilage stretches like a thick rubber band. Some of it can be found where our bones come together. Cartilage is in between the discs which run up our back. It can even be found on the tip of our noses and on the outside of our ears.

This body tape is tough and strong. It isn't as hard as bone but it is lasting.

Cartilage has two helpers which do the same type of job. Ligaments and tendons also tape our bones together. These two do not stretch but act more like strong cables or ropes.

The easiest place to find a tendon is to feel behind your ankle. This is your largest tendon. It holds the muscles in your calf to your heel.

If you stand on your toes you can feel this tendon tighten. This tape not only holds our bones together but it helps us push, step, walk and run forward.

These tapes help us reach and stretch without throwing our bones out of joint. They also give us a great deal of comfort. If there were no cartilage between the discs in our back, the bones would keep hitting and make it too painful for us to walk.

Often athletes, especially football players, tear the cartilage in their knee. When this happens surgery is usually needed since cartilage does not heal well.

It would not be much fun to move around without this body tape. We would have trouble walking, reaching or moving at all.

Many years ago the Apostle Paul was discussing how people can get along with each other. What can tape us together and still allow us to stretch?

What would work like cartilage, ligaments and tendons?

Paul decided there was only one thing; it had to be love. By loving each other we can avoid arguing and fighting. By loving each other we stop "rubbing" each other wrong. There are fewer bumps and less misunderstandings.

Christ's special tape is the same as Paul's. They taught us to love relatives, friends, neighbors and even enemies.

"This is what I have asked of God for you: that you will be encouraged and knit together by strong ties of love, and that you will have the rich experience of knowing Christ with real certainty and clear understanding" (Col. 2:2, TLB).

1. What is body tape?
2. How does cartilage help our discs?
3. What is God's tape for people?

Love is better than hurting each other.

forty-five

Muscles Are Amazing

 How many push-ups can you do? Maybe you can't do any yet, but you will. Possibly you can do 10, 20, 50 or even 100.

One day a 16-year-old boy started doing push-ups. Charles Linster was used to doing long exercises, so he thought he would try something especially hard. He wanted to see how many push-ups he could do without stopping.

Three hours and 54 minutes later Linster had completed 6,006 push-ups. No one had ever done this many before without stopping.

We are probably never going to come close to this, but it is amazing what our muscles can do. If we practice we can soon increase the number of push-ups, chin-ups or sit-ups we can do.

How does a muscle work? We know we have them even though they are hidden under our skin. We also know you can become stronger by using ͵our muscles. But what really makes them operate?

Suppose you pick up a chair or a bag of groceries. Immediately your muscles go to work. Much of our muscles are made up of capillaries. These capillaries just rest most of the time. But when you need muscle, blood comes rushing into the capillaries. They grow larger immediately. Sometimes they jump to 800 times their resting size.

When your muscles call for this much blood, your heart will have to beat faster to get it moving. If your heart is going to beat faster, you will have to breathe harder. Your body will need oxygen to make this machine run at top speed.

Most parts of our body will need two muscles. A muscle does many great things but there is one thing it can't do. Muscles can pull but cannot push. There is a muscle to help us look to the left. However, that muscle cannot turn our eye to the right because it can't push. A second muscle is needed to switch the eye to the right.

A set of muscles lift your arms. They can't lower them. A second set takes care of that job.

When you smile, one set of muscles lifts your face. Are you finished? It will take a second set to let your smile down again.

Muscles are not only great for strength, but even come in handy for producing heat. If you are in a chilly room sometime, get down and do 15 push-ups. Your body will heat up to supply your muscles. They will also heat the rest of your body and have some heat left over to warm up the room just a little.

The rush of blood makes it possible for us to have quick physical strength. With it we can do amazing things. There are other times when we need another type of strength. We need to be strong enough to keep from doing something wrong. We need to be strong enough to be kind when others are being mean. We even need to be strong when we are disappointed and don't get our way.

Jesus Christ wants to help by giving us this strength. Our muscles can't do it but Christ can.

"For I can do everything God asks me to do with the help of Christ who gives me the strength and power" (Phil. 4:13, TLB).

1. Why do we need "pairs" of muscles?
2. How many push-ups can you do?
3. What does Christ want to make you strong for?

I want to be strong enough to do what is right.

forty-six

Left-handed

 The Old Testament tells us about a special group of people. They had been chosen because they could do something better than anyone else. Seven hundred men had been selected because they were especially good with their left hand.

The Israelites had a small army of men who were skillful with their slings. These slings were used to throw a stone hard enough to knock out a grown man. Because of the way these slings were made, it was easier to use them if you were left-handed.

These 700 men were selected because they were excellent shots with their left hand. They were so good, the Bible tells us, that almost every time they could hit a target within a "hair's width" (Judges 20:16).

Left-handed children used to get picked on by many people. Their parents sometimes tried to make them use their right hand. Teachers used to take the child's pen and push it into his right hand. Often the person would pick up the nickname "Lefty" and even his friends would tease him.

Today this feeling has changed. In many classes there are probably two or three students who are left-handed. Some people believe that there are more left-handed people today than there were 20 years ago. This is because today there are less attempts to make everyone right-handed.

It's all right to be different. One person likes to read while another person likes to play basketball. Many people like both. A few students enjoy taking tests; other students hate them. Some people feel comfortable using their left hand while others don't. It's okay. Either way works out great.

How does someone become left-handed? It is hard to say. Some people are just "born" left-handed. We call this being "naturally" left-handed.

The same thing is true in the plant world. One type of plant will grow up a pole always from the left. Another type of plant will always circle the pole from the right.

However, even though a child isn't born left-handed he may enjoy using his left hand more than his right. As children watch their parents or friends, they may also choose to be left-handed.

Usually if both parents are left-handed the child will be the same. But not necessarily. Many become right-handed.

Often attempts to make a left-handed person right-handed have caused only harm. The person has not felt comfortable and in many cases has returned to being left-handed.

We used to think left-handed people would have a hard life. Pencil sharpeners were made for right-handed people. It looked as though left-handed people could not write well. They often seemed to be poking the person next to them at the table.

Today we know better. Being left-handed doesn't hurt anyone. The truth is that some of the most outstanding figures in history were left-handed. Leonardo da Vinci, Harry Truman, Picasso and Michaelangelo were just a few.

Baseball fans like to argue over who was the greatest batter of all time. Was it Ty Cobb, Babe Ruth, Ted Williams, Stan Musial, Mickey Mantle, Pete Rose? Take your pick. They *all* batted left-handed.

God doesn't worry about who is left-handed or right-handed. He is more concerned with whether we decide to use those hands for good or bad. He wants to know if we use our hands to hurt people or help them. That type of decision is made inside a person. The important thing is how we feel about other people and about God.

When God looks for a person to do His work, He doesn't care if he is left-handed.

"But when they cried to the Lord, he sent them a savior, Ehud (son of Gera, a Benjaminite), who was left-handed" (Judges 3:15, TLB).

1. Why are people left-handed?
2. Name three famous left-handed people.
3. Who does God like best—right-handed or left-handed people?

I am not better. I am not worse. I am glad to be me.

forty-seven

The Pressure Inside

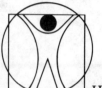 Have you ever had a doctor or nurse wrap a rubber tube around your arm? He then pumped air into it to make the tube tight. This is called checking your blood pressure.

The heart carries on a big job of pumping blood. Not only must it pump blood often but it must pump it hard enough. If the blood is being pushed too hard or too weakly, our body could have troubles.

Most of the time the doctor is looking for two things. First he wants to know how hard the blood pushes during the heartbeat. Then he checks to see what it is like between beats.

It is no easy job to push blood quickly throughout a human body. Some of our blood vessels are thinner than hair.

How hard the blood needs to pump may depend on the size and health of the person. What may be all right for one individual could be dangerous for another. Young children usually have lower blood pressure than young adults or the elderly.

In order to do its job properly the blood must move quickly. It races through our arteries at about 100 feet per minute. Blood has to hurry back to the heart so it can start the trip again.

Blood pressure will increase under a number of conditions. If danger comes, our blood pumps harder. When we work or play the pressure increases. If we weigh too much, the blood has to work harder. For most people worry will also make it work too much.

If a person's blood pressure is too high for too long, he could be in danger. Over a long time the heart becomes overworked. The blood vessels find it difficult to handle so much pressure. This problem seems to increase after the age of 35.

Part of the problems of blood pressure come from too much tension. We worry over a long period of time. After years of this our heart and body grow tired and often weak.

Many people have been able to relax more by giving their worries to Jesus Christ. Not all of our cares go away but many of them can. It is great to know someone else cares and can help.

"Let him have all your worries and cares, for he is always thinking about you and watching everything that concerns you" (1 Pet. 5:7, TLB).

1. How thin are some blood vessels?
2. At what age does the blood pressure problem increase?
3. Name one thing that sometimes worries you.

Keep us calm by remembering you care.

forty-eight

What Type of Blood?

 Have you ever needed someone else's blood? Every year five million people in the United States lose some of their blood and need to be resupplied from another person. This is called a transfusion.

Getting blood from another person isn't hard to do if it is done correctly, but there are dangers. If doctors didn't know what they were doing, the wrong blood could cause death.

If you ever need an operation, you may be glad blood transfusions are possible. Not too long ago some operations were impossible because of the loss of blood. A hard working doctor named Karl Landsteiner was a big help when he found out there are different types of blood.

Because of the work of Dr. Landsteiner and others blood transfusions have been used often since World War II.

Most people have one of these four types of blood: A, B, AB or O. There are probably twenty types altogether but these four are the most common. If we need blood during an operation or after an accident, the doctor will make sure we get the right kind.

After the doctor checks to see what type of blood you have, he has to ask a second question. Is your Rh factor positive or negative? About 85% of all people are Rh positive. The rest of the population is Rh negative. Those who are negative cannot receive blood from those who are positive.

Before blood types were discovered, safe transfusions were impossible. Today, because of well-trained doctors we can get the blood we need.

When we need blood we often must have it immediately. There may not be time to ask friends to give theirs. This is why there are "blood banks." The blood is collected from volunteer donors and kept until needed.

Blood cannot be made except in a human body. Most healthy people can donate blood four times each year.

Even those who are in perfect health, however, need someone else's blood. They don't need a transfusion but they need the blood of Jesus Christ, God's Son, to pay for their sins. That's why Jesus died on the cross.

No one else could do that for us.

"But he paid for you with the precious lifeblood of Christ, the sinless, spotless Lamb of God" (1 Pet. 1:19, TLB).

1. What are the four main types of blood?
2. How many people in the United States lose some of their blood and need a new supply?
3. What did Christ's blood do for us?

The blood of Christ has cleansed us.

forty-nine

Living Longer

While looking at a magazine, I wondered what it would be like to live in another country. The pictures were beautiful, especially the scenery. However, the people lived in straw huts and slept on the ground. Food was hard to get and everyone looked dirty. The article said the average person lived to be 32 years old.

After reading those facts, the country didn't seem so interesting. In nations where there are good food, warm homes and healthy bodies, we expect to live much longer. A baby born today can live for as long as 70 years or more.

This is a big increase in years lived since 1900. Many babies died then because of diseases. If you visit an old cemetery you will see a large number of headstones marking the graves of babies and young mothers. Today we are healthier and can expect to live much longer.

For most of us the biggest health problems we will face later are cancer and heart disease. Scientists are working hard to stop both of these "killers." If they are successful your children or grandchildren may live to be 120 years old. They won't just be older, they will be healthier also.

When we take better care of our bodies we live longer. Most of us eat better than people did a hundred years ago. Fresh fruit and milk give us good vitamins.

Better medical attention has given life to children and adults who would otherwise have died. An infected appendix would have killed someone before, but now it is easily removed. A disease called smallpox previously killed hundreds of thousands of people, but now this disease is rare. Years ago many mothers died while giving birth to children, but science has greatly helped and deaths at birth are few.

The attention given to physical exercise will probably help many of us to live longer.

However, there is more to life than many years or even good health. For someone to get the most out of life, he needs to know and follow Jesus Christ. Life isn't complete if we're concerned only about the body and the mind. Our whole person must be correctly related to God.

"And Jesus answered him, saying, It is written, That man shall not live by bread alone, but by every word of God" (Luke 4:4, KJV).

1. What are the biggest health problems?
2. If scientists are successful, how long might you live?
3. Where can we find God's words?

Thanks for a full life with you.

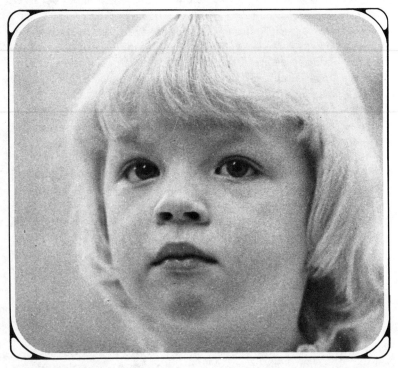

fifty
Speaking Well

Can you say "The ball bounces better on blacktop"? If you were able to pronounce these words clearly, you should be extremely happy. There are many children who have trouble forming their lips correctly. Some sounds are too hard to pronounce.

Now try another test. How many words can you say while holding your two lips stiff and not allowing them to touch? Many words are impossible to repeat.

We often see children who have this problem. When some children are born their upper lip has not grown together. Maybe the roof of their mouth did not finish forming either. This is called a cleft lip or cleft palate.

Before the child was born, something went wrong in his body. Many children are born without something. Often a child is born without all his tooth buds. He won't have all 32 teeth. Some children are missing a toe or a small finger. It isn't unheard of to have an extra toe.

In the case of the cleft lip or palate, something has gone wrong and will now have to be fixed. Some babies with this problem must be fed carefully to stop the food from backing up into the nose.

As bad as all this sounds, there is great hope through the work of excellent doctors. As early as possible they will repair the child's lip and consider the palate or roof. Some doctors specialize in cleft palate problems. Several of them may work as a team and can repair extremely serious cases.

Afterwards dentists will make special teeth for the child. Speech teachers are then able to teach the young person to pronounce difficult words more smoothly.

Too often the person who faces this problem has an added heartache. Some children aren't careful and start teasing and calling him names. It is hard enough for him without people giving him a bad time. Christian children could help by refusing to tease him or anyone else with a handicap.

The important thing is not the shape of our lips but rather how we use them. The person with perfectly formed lips can use them as knives to stab others. Kinder people use lips to speak well of each other.

God is concerned about the way I talk. He knows how much good my words can do.

"Set a watch, O Lord, before my mouth; keep the door of my lips" (Ps. 141:3, KJV).

1. How are cleft palates fixed?
2. What is the roof of your mouth called?
3. Name three nice things we could say to cheer up someone.

Kind words make good medicine.

fifty-one

The Alarm System

 "I think we will have to remove Johnny's tonsils," said the kind doctor. "If we don't, he is going to be sick and probably miss a lot of school."

Most of us have heard of tonsils because so many children have had them removed. But what is their purpose? How do they do their job? Why are they sometimes taken out?

Tonsils make a good alarm system to warn our body if something dangerous is coming. They are located in the back of the mouth and can be seen easily by a doctor. When we eat, pieces of food touch the small dots on our tonsils. If there is something harmful in the food the rest of our body is alerted right away, "Here comes trouble."

Immediately our body goes to work to fight the danger. In most cases our system overcomes the problem and keeps us in good health.

But if tonsils are so helpful, why are so many removed by doctors? In some cases they do not do their job. Instead of fighting sickness the tonsils become filled with harmful particles. When this happens, our tonsils start hurting us instead of helping.

Soon this person gets many sore throats. He begins missing school because his body is run-down. It is filled with infection. The tonsils themselves may become extra large. Added infection spreads through the body.

When the tonsils do more harm than good, the doctor may decide to remove them. For many children it is a minor operation. Usually they spend a few days in the hospital and later get to eat lots of ice cream.

Some children have large tonsils but don't need to have them removed. If they are not infected, they sometimes shrink as the child grows older.

If there are repeated sore throats and general sickness, a smart family contacts the doctor. Trying to guess about your tonsils' condition could lead to greater illness.

Warning systems are important. Some of us have bought fire-alarm systems for our homes to help protect us. God put many good warning signals in our body. He also gave us an excellent system to guide the rest of our lives.

A great deal of the Bible is written to warn us. Sin will hurt people. Selfishness can make someone sad. Gossip can ruin someone's name. If we read the Bible, it can let us know what things to stay away from.

"For they warn us away from harm and give success to those who obey them" (Ps. 19:11, TLB).

1. Why do some children have to have their tonsils out?
2. Where are our tonsils located?
3. Name one warning in the Bible.

Some warnings are great for protecting us.

fifty-two

Growing Up Quickly

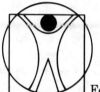 For a long time Ann was a little girl, but at 13 she began changing. Her body looked different and her voice wasn't quite the same. The same thing happened to Allen. When he was 14 his voice sounded different. He started to get a little more hair on his body.

What has happened to Ann and Allen? The same thing which happens to all of us. They have started a part of their lives called puberty. Their bodies are beginning to change and soon they will be young adults.

This important change starts somewhere between the ages of 12 and 17. We shouldn't be too concerned if it doesn't though. A few people begin puberty earlier and some later than this.

Often these changes will begin earlier in girls since their bodies grow differently from boys' bodies. The most noticeable change will be in the development of breasts. This is early preparation for being a mother. The organs inside a girl's body are also getting ready to some day carry a child. Tiny eggs which have been stored in special places called ovaries since the time she was born begin to mature one at a time. Before a girl is ready to be a mother, this mature egg along with the lining materials of the uterus (the organ where babies grow) passes out of her body monthly.

It is an exciting time. Although the changes are sometimes confusing for a girl, she learns to like it. She starts to get hair under her arms and in her pubic area. Some girls will also get a little hair on their face. Usually they will begin to spend more time in front of a mirror, working on their appearance.

For boys puberty is just as interesting, although the changes may not be as easily seen. Boys get little whiskers on their face. They also get hair under their arms and in the pubic area. Some boys get hair on their chest, but most don't. The word puberty means "to become hairy."

The pitch of a boy's voice will usually drop from high to low. During this time his voice will often do funny things. In the middle of a sentence his voice might suddenly crack, jumping to a high squeak. Later it will settle down again.

Often a boy's body will change also. Sometimes his hips will become smaller and his shoulders broader. This isn't always the case though, and should not worry the boy.

The boy's body becomes different inside. Soon it will start to produce sperm. This is preparation for being a father.

Most people find puberty a good part of life when they realize what is happening to them. Leaving childhood behind, puberty becomes the doorstep to becoming adults. During this time young people make more decisions and enjoy new things.

Behavior habits also change and become more mature. Young people can undertake more responsibility. They usually don't do the foolish things they used to do. They are growing up and it can be seen in their behavior.

"It's like this: when I was a child I spoke and thought and reasoned as a child does. But when I became a man my thoughts grew far beyond those of my childhood and now I have put away the childish things" (1 Cor. 13:11, TLB).

1. What is puberty?
2. At what age does puberty start?
3. What good changes in behavior come with puberty?

We aren't adults until we act like adults.